AF695122

The Right to Democracy in International Law

This book explores the right to democracy in international law and contemporary democratic theory, asking whether international law encompasses a substantive or procedural understanding of the notion. The book considers whether there can be considered to be a basis for the right to democracy in international customary law through identification of the relevant State practice and *opinio juris*, as well as through an evaluation of the Universal Declaration of Human Rights and whether the relevant provisions might be interpreted as forming customary law. The book then goes on to explore the relevant provisions in international treaties including the International Covenant on Civil and Political Rights before looking at the role of regional organizations and human rights regimes including the European Court of Human Rights and the Arab human rights regime. Khalifa A. Alfadhel draws on the work of John Rawls in order to put forward a theoretical basis for the right to democracy.

Khalifa A. Alfadhel is an Assistant Professor of Public International Law at the University of Bahrain.

Routledge Research in International Law

For details of the full series please visit:
https://www.routledge.com/series/SCLW49

Available:

The Rule of Law in the UN Security Council
Turning the Focus Inwards
Sherif Elgebeily

Forthcoming titles in this series include:

Technology and the Law on the Use of Force
New Security Challenges in the Twenty First Century
Jackson Maogoto

International Law and the Rights of those Displaced by Armed Conflict
Elena Katselli Proukaki

International Criminal Law and Sexual Violence against Women
The Interpretation of Gender in the Contemporary International Criminal Trial
Daniela Nadj

Fighting and Victimhood in International Criminal Law
Joanna Nicholson

Human Security Discourse and International Law
A Principled Approach
Shireen Daft

Queering International Law
Possibilities, Alliances, Complicities, Risks
Dianne Otto

The Right to Democracy in International Law

Between Procedure, Substance and the Philosophy of John Rawls

Khalifa A. Alfadhel

Routledge
Taylor & Francis Group
LONDON AND NEW YORK

First published 2017 by Routledge

2 Park Square, Milton Park, Abingdon, Oxfordshire OX14 4RN
52 Vanderbilt Avenue, New York, NY 10017

Routledge is an imprint of the Taylor & Francis Group, an informa business

First issued in paperback 2018

Copyright © 2017 Khalifa A. Alfadhel

The right of Khalifa A. Alfadhel to be identified as author of this work has been asserted by him in accordance with sections 77 and 78 of the Copyright, Designs and Patents Act 1988.

All rights reserved. No part of this book may be reprinted or reproduced or utilised in any form or by any electronic, mechanical, or other means, now known or hereafter invented, including photocopying and recording, or in any information storage or retrieval system, without permission in writing from the publishers.

Notice:
Product or corporate names may be trademarks or registered trademarks, and are used only for identification and explanation without intent to infringe.

British Library Cataloguing in Publication Data
A catalogue record for this book is available from the British Library

Library of Congress Cataloging in Publication Data
A catalog record for this book has been requested

ISBN: 978-1-138-29443-1 (hbk)
ISBN: 978-0-367-19347-8 (pbk)

Typeset in Times New Roman
by Apex CoVantage, LLC

To H.A.K.

Contents

Table of international law xi
Table of international cases xiii
Abbreviations xv

Introduction 1

1 The Refah *principle and democratic theory 7*
2 Limitations 10
3 Structure and methodology 10

1 The right to democracy in international customary law 13

1.1 Introduction 13
1.2 The right to democracy in traditional international customary law 15
1.3 The right to democracy in modern international customary law: the Universal Declaration of Human Rights 17
a The legal value of the Universal Declaration of Human Rights 18
b Article 21: between *travaux préparatoires* and substance 22
1.4 A monitoring mechanism? 25
1.5 Conclusion 27

2 The right to democracy in international conventions – the International Covenant on Civil and Political Rights 29

2.1 Introduction 29
2.2 Context, background and derogations 31
2.3 The Human Rights Committee 33
2.4 Article 25: the right to political participation 36
a A right of citizens 38
b The right to vote 39
c The right to stand 43
2.5 Conclusion 48

3 The substantive right to democracy in international law 49

3.1 Introduction 49
3.2 Procedural shortcomings 52
3.3 The role of international organizations 55
3.4 The role of regional organizations and the European Court of Human Rights 59
3.5 Conclusion: substance or procedure? 63

4 Democracy and the citizen in the philosophy of John Rawls 66

4.1 Introduction 66
4.2 Liberty behind a veil of ignorance 67
4.3 The reasonable citizen 73
4.4 The overlapping consensus 75
4.5 Public reason 78
4.6 An escape from liberty 81
4.7 Conclusion 90

Conclusion 93

1 Summary 93
2 The law: incomplete procedural understanding of democracy 93
3 Democratic theory: needs to be extended 94

Bibliography 97
Index 105

This will always remain one of the best jokes of democracy, that it gave its deadly enemies the means by which it was destroyed.

– Joseph Goebbels, Nazi Minister of Propaganda.

Table of international law

Charter of the United Nations 1945 Art 64 25
Declaration of the Rights of Man and of Citizen 1789....24
Declaration on Criteria for Free and Fair Elections 1994 52
Art 2....53
European Convention for the Protection of Human Rights and Fundamental Freedoms 1950 59
Art 3....61
Art 11....8, 61
European Union Treaty on European Union (Consolidated Version), Treaty of Maastricht 1992....59
International Covenant on Civil and Political Rights 1966....1, 6, 10, 13, 17, 29, 31, 32, 33, 34, 35, 37, 38, 41, 47, 48, 52, 55
Art 1....29
Art 2....42
Art 4....31, 32
Art 6....29
Art 8....29
Art 14....30
Art 19....46
Art 21....30, 33, 49, 88
Art 25....30, 32, 33, 36, 37, 38, 39, 40, 42, 43, 44, 45, 46, 47, 48, 49, 93
Art 28....33
Art 32....33
Art 40....33, 35
Art 41....33
International Covenant on Economic, Social and Cultural Rights 1966....17
Organization of African Unity Constitutive Act of the African Union 2000....60
Organization of American States Protocol of Amendments to the Charter of the Organization of American States 1992....59
Statute of the International Court of Justice....21
Art 38....1, 10, 15, 21, 30
Universal Declaration of Human Rights 1948, ...1, 6, 10, 13, 15, 17, 18, 19, 20, 21, 25, 26, 27, 29, 30, 31, 52, 53
Art 1....2, 22
Art 2....4
Art 4....22

Art 5 ... 22
Art 17 ... 31
Art 21 ... 3, 10, 14, 15, 18, 22, 23, 24, 25, 27, 28, 36, 49, 93
Art 25 ... 2, 3, 4, 5, 49
Art 29 ... 25, 32
Vienna Convention on the Law of Treaties 1969 ... 31

Table of international cases

Bandaranayake v Sri Lanka, Communication No. 1376/2007, 24 July 2008. CCPR/C/93/D/1376/2005 ... 46
Bwalya v Zambia, Communication No. 314/1988, 27 July 1993. CCPR/C/48/D/314/1988 ... 43
Debreczeny v Netherlands, Communication No. 500/1992, 3 April 1995. CCPR/C/53/D/500/1992 ... 47
Diergaardt et al. v Namibia, Communication No. 760/1997, 25 July 2000. CCPR/C/69/D/760/1997 ... 46
Dissanayake. Sri Lanka, Communication No. 1373/2005, 22 July 2005. CCPR/C/93/D/1373/2005 ... 46
Fisheries Jurisdiction Case (Federal Republic of Germany v Iceland) (Merits) [1973] ICJ Rep 56 ... 16
Gillot v France, Communication No. 932/2000, 26 July 2002. CCPR/C/75/D/932/2000 ... 47
Handyside v United Kingdom, Series A No. 24 (1979/80) ... 60
Herri Batasuna v Spain (Apps 25803/04 & 25817/04) Judgment of the Grand Chamber of 30 June 2009 ... 63
Ignatane v Latvia, Communication No. 884/1999, 31 July 2001. CCPR/C/72/D/884/1999 ... 46
Jacobs v Belgium, Communication No. 943/2000, 17 August 2004. CCPR/C/81/D/943/2000 ... 47
Jersild v Denmark, Series A No. 298 (1994) ... 60
Jong-Cheol v Republic of Korea, Communication No. 968/2001, 27 July 2005. CCPR/C/84/D/968/2001 ... 46
Korneenko v Belarus, Communication No. 1226/2003, 20 July 2012. CCPR/C/105/D/1226/2003 ... 45
Matyus v Slovakia, Communication No. 923/2000, 22 July 2002. CCPR/C/75/D/923/2000 ... 40
Mazou v Cameroon, Communication No. 630/1995, 3 August 2001. CCPR/C/72/D/630/1995 ... 46
North Sea Continental Shelf Cases (Federal Republic of Germany v Denmark; Federal Republic of Germany v Netherlands) (Merits) [1969] ICJ Rep 52 ... 16

Paksas v Lithuania, Communication No. 2155/2012, 21 March 2014. CCPR/C/110/D/2155/2012 ... 45
Paraga v Croatia, Communication No. 727/1996, 4 April 2001. CCPR/C/71/D/727/1996 ... 46
Refah Partisi (Welfare Party) and others v Turkey (Apps. 41340/98, 41342/98 and 41344/98), Judgment of the Grand Chamber of 13 February 2003 ... 7, 61, 62, 63, 64, 67, 75, 76, 78, 94
SS Lotus, 1927 PCIJ Series A, No. 10 ... 35
United Communist Party of Turkey and Others v Turkey (App. 19392/92), Judgment of 30 January 1998 (1998) ... 61

Abbreviations

AJIL	American Journal of International Law
AU	African Union
ECHR	European Convention on Human Rights
ECtHR	European Court of Human Rights
EJIL	European Journal of International Law
HRC	Human Rights Committee
ICCPR	International Covenant on Civil and Political Rights
ICJ	International Court of Justice
ICLQ	International and Comparative Law Quarterly
ILM	International Legal Material
OAS	Organization of American States
UDHR	Universal Declaration of Human Rights
UN	United Nations
UNGA	UN General Assembly

Introduction

The right to democracy in international law is certainly an emerging one. With reference to the sources of international law as stipulated in Article 38 of the Statute of the International Court of Justice (ICJ), this book will identify the position of the right in question with relation to international customary law, international conventions and the relevant works of notable scholars.[1] The main assumption is that the right to democracy does not reflect international custom, with reference to State practice and *opinio juris*. In assessing the modern customary approach, one could also find that the right in question is not compelling in the context of the Universal Declaration of Human Rights (UDHR).[2] The content of the democracy norm in the context of the Declaration is a procedural one, limited to the conduct of periodic free and fair elections on a periodic basis.

The pattern continues in the assessment of the position of the right to democracy in international and regional conventions. The International Covenant on Civil and Political Rights (ICCPR) also reflects a procedural understanding.[3] A richer substantive understanding of the term was

1 Article 38 (1) of the Statute of the ICJ states:

1 The Court, whose function is to decide in accordance with international law such disputes as are submitted to it, shall apply:
   a international conventions, whether general or particular, establishing rules expressly recognized by the contesting states;
   b international custom, as evidence of a general practice accepted as law;
   c the general principles of law recognized by civilized nations;
   d subject to the provisions of Article 59, judicial decisions and the teachings of the most highly qualified publicists of the various nations, as subsidiary means for the determination of rules of law.

2 Universal Declaration of Human Rights (adopted 10 December 1948) UNGA Res 217 A (III) UN Doc A/810 (hereinafter UDHR).

3 International Covenant on Civil and Political Rights (adopted 16 December 1966. Entered into force 3 January 1976) UNGA Res 2200A (XXI) UN Doc A/6316 999 UNTS 171; (1967) 6 *ILM* 368.

advanced by a number of international instruments, however, without any significant support by State practice and international organizations.

The idea of an entitlement to democracy first found itself in the literature of international law in the post-Soviet era. Thomas Franck was one of the first pioneers of this conception.[4] The idea of the collapse of the Soviet Bloc led some to believe that the World was ready to reach the final steps of political evolution, and the time had come to celebrate the 'end of history' through the global adoption of democracy as a form of government.[5] However this is far from being the case.

Franck came with the idea of the democratic entitlement in the beginning of the 1990s. His position comes from a point that is rooted in the exercise of self-determination in international law and derived from the American Declaration of Independence that was the starting point of his argument.[6] Franck articulates: '[s]elf-determination postulates the right of a people organised in an established territory to determine its collective political destiny in a democratic fashion and is therefore at the core of the democratic entitlement.'[7]

There is a considerable amount of literature on the relation between the right to self-determination and the right to political participation.[8] However, this book shares the view of the Human Rights Committee (HRC) on the distinctive character of each right. The Committee provided in its General Comment 25: '[t]he rights under article 25 [the right to vote and to be elected] are related to, but distinct from, the right of peoples to self-determination. By virtue of the rights covered by article 1 (1), peoples have

4 TM Franck, 'The Emerging Right to Democratic Governance' (1992) 86 *AJIL* 46.

5 See F Fukuyama, *The End of History and the Last Man* (Penguin 1993).

6 Franck (n 4) 48–9. For a detailed analysis and critique on Franck's article, see R Burchill, 'The Developing International Law of Democracy' (2001) 1 *Modern Law Review* 123, 127–30.

7 Franck, ibid 52.

8 Some commentators associated the democratic entitlement with internal and external self-determination. For the internal aspect of the hypothesis see BR Roth, *Governmental Illegitimacy in International Law* (Oxford University Press 2000); S Wheatley, 'Deliberative Democracy and Minorities' (2003) 14 *EJIL* 507; S Wheatley, *Democracy, Minorities and International Law* (Cambridge University Press 2005); J d'Aspremont, 'Legitimacy of Governments in the Age of Democracy' (2006) 38 *New York University Journal of International Law and Politics* 877; J d'Aspremont, 'Responsibility for Coups in International Law' (2010) 18 *Tulane Journal of International and Comparative Law* 451. As for the association of the term with external self-determination, see R Rich, 'Recognition of States: The Collapse of Yugoslavia and the Soviet Union' (1993) 4 *EJIL* 36; S Murphy, 'Democratic Legitimacy and the Recognition of States and Governments' (1999) 48 *ICLQ* 545; J Vidmar, *Democratic Statehood in International Law: The Emergence of New States in Post-Cold War Practice* (Hart 2013).

the right to freely determine their political status and to enjoy the right to choose the form of their constitution or government. Article 25 deals with the right of individuals to participate in those processes which constitute the conduct of public affairs. Those rights, as individual rights, can give rise to claims under the first Optional Protocol.'[9] Hence, the right to political participation (democracy) is an individual right, while the right of peoples to self-determination is collective. Therefore, the democratic entitlement is a literary concept rather than a legal one. It fails to address the issue of the nature of the right to democracy, and makes a serious conflict of conceptions. Also, the right to self-determination (in all of its aspects) is concretely rooted in international law, where State practice was consistent, rather than the right in question, which is still emerging in the wrong direction.

Considering the sources of international law as provided in the Statute of the ICJ, a question arises: does the right to democracy reflect international customary law? The answer to this will be (mainly) in assessing the position of the notion in the context of the UDHR.

Article 21 of the Declaration provided:

1 Everyone has the right to take part in the government of his country, directly or through freely chosen representatives.
2 Everyone has the right of equal access to public service in his country.
3 The will of the people shall be the basis of the authority of government; this will shall be expressed in periodic and genuine elections which shall be by universal and equal suffrage and shall be held by secret vote or by equivalent free voting procedures.

In order to answer the question regarding the position of the right to democracy in the context of international customary law, the book will assess the classical approach in recognizing international custom through the identification of State practice accompanied by *opinio juris*; followed by the consideration of the modern customary approach based in international declarations, where the UDHR stands as a significant instrument in this respect.[10] The assessment will conclude that there is no international customary law reflected in this setting, and the relevant provision in the

9 General Comment No. 25: *The right to participate in public affairs, voting rights and the right of equal access to public service* (Art. 25): 12/07/1996. CCPR/C/21/Rev.1/Add.7 para. 2.

10 The UDHR will be assessed in this setting since it reflects the idea of modern declarative customary law as advanced by a number of commentators. See AE Roberts, 'Traditional and Modern Approaches to Customary International Law: A Reconciliation' (2001) 95 *AJIL* 757.

Declaration reflects a procedural understanding that is insufficient in applying sustainable democratic governance in transitional societies.

A second question arises with regard to the sources of international law: is the right to democracy reflected in international conventions? The answer to this will be in the context of the ICCPR. The procedural view extends in Article 25 of the Covenant which states:

> Every citizen shall have the right and the opportunity, without any of the distinctions mentioned in article 2 and without unreasonable restrictions:
>
> (a) To take part in the conduct of public affairs, directly or through freely chosen representatives;
> (b) To vote and to be elected at genuine periodic elections which shall be by universal and equal suffrage and shall be held by secret ballot, guaranteeing the free expression of the will of the electors;
> (c) To have access, on general terms of equality, to public service in his country.

Together with the corresponding Article in the UDHR, the aforementioned provision does not have any reference to the foundational pillars of democracy, such as pluralism, public reason and the overlapping consensus necessary to establish a democratic society. The HRC does not significantly contribute to the development of a right to democracy in international law beyond the procedural understanding. The Committee provided in General Comment 25:

> Whatever form of constitution or government is in force, the Covenant requires States to adopt such legislative and other measures as may be necessary to ensure that citizens have an effective opportunity to enjoy the rights it protects.

From the previous, one could safely conclude that the HRC does not set out positive measures on State parties to the Covenant to adopt a substantive form of democratic government. The pattern continues in the jurisprudence of the Committee, which only affirmed the procedural aspect of democracy in all individual communications associated with Article 25.[11] Therefore, the procedural right to democracy as stipulated in the context of the ICCPR

11 A detailed assessment of the jurisprudence associated with Article 25 of the ICCPR will be presented in Chapter 2 of this book.

is not a concrete (human) right subject to specific terms of reference, rather, an international codification of a minimalist electoral model, subject to wide State discretion.

From the assessment of the right to democracy in the context of Article 25 of the ICCPR, one could reach the following conclusions:

1 The text of the relevant provision and the jurisprudence of the HRC do not provide any detailed elaboration on the nature, scope and role of the citizen, who is the first unit of a democratic society. It emphasizes that democracy is a citizen's right, without any reference to the requirement of reasonableness that is necessary to avoid the rise of political intolerance based on comprehensive moral/religious doctrines.
2 The focus on the procedural element is a significant conceptual problem, where the right to democracy needs to extend beyond the thin electoral model, in order to be an end in itself where other fundamental rights and freedoms are endorsed and protected, not as a means to reach power and subsequently abolish the democratic system.

Gregory Fox was a pioneering scholar who catalogued the right to democracy in international law to two categories: procedural and substantive.[12] The procedural understanding of the right is limited to the conduct of free and fair elections on a periodic basis,[13] while the substantive account sees the notion as a series of mutually reinforcing rights.[14] The substantive account of the right to democracy in international law views democracy as a means to enforce other individual rights and freedoms.[15] The right to democracy is not 'absolute' in the sense that it could eliminate itself or abolish other fundamental political and civil freedoms.[16] The procedural view – as mentioned earlier – is limited to periodic free and fair elections, where it regulates 'decision-making but does not prescribe the decisions themselves'.[17] This contrast, and assessment, to the precise aspect of political intolerance makes one important assumption, which is that, the procedural understanding of the right to democracy makes the right toothless against anti-democratic

12 GH Fox, 'Democracy, Right to, International Protection' in R Wolfrum (ed.), *Max Planck Encyclopedia of Public International Law* (Oxford University Press 2013). Also see GH Fox and BR Roth (eds), *Democratic Governance and International Law* (Cambridge University Press 2000).
13 Fox, *Democracy, Right to* para. 5.
14 Ibid.
15 Fox (n 12) 16.
16 Ibid.
17 Ibid 14.

actors. In other words, the entitlement to periodic free and fair elections does not necessarily mean a right to democracy.

The substantive account of democracy is found in the consideration of wider developments in international law. This is with reference to a number of reports delivered by the UN Secretary-General, declarations issued by the General Assembly and other international bodies. The Vienna Declaration and Programme of Action provided:

> Democracy, development and respect for human rights and fundamental freedoms are interdependent and mutually reinforcing. Democracy is based on the freely expressed will of the people to determine their own political, economic, social and cultural systems and their full participation in all aspects of their lives.[18]

The substantive account of the right to democracy affords a richer understanding of the term, linking the notion to a number of mutually reinforcing rights, and necessary for the maintenance and sustainability of, democracy. The substantive account does indeed contribute positively in the development of a human right to democracy in international law. However, the application of the substantive account 'alone' would not lead to the full realization of democratic triumph without the consideration of the theoretical elements of the notion, especially, those associated with the citizen.

From the above, an important question arises with the observance of international law's protection of a right to democratic government regarding the conceptual nature of the right involved: does international law encompass a substantive or procedural understanding of the notion? In answering this, one can safely say that the latter understanding supersedes. This is because State practice and the behaviour of international organizations did not provide a prompt delivery of the substantive account. The promotion, monitoring and execution of the right in question does not centrally extend beyond election monitoring, capacity building and technical assistance associated with the 'procedures' of democracy. However, the nature and content of the procedural understanding remains vague and unclear based on the jurisprudence of the HRC, and even in the democratic provisions in the UDHR and ICCPR. Therefore, such limitation remains the biggest obstacle towards the enforcement of a comprehensive right to democratic governance. The current position of the right to democracy in international law reflects an

18 UNGA, *Vienna Declaration and Programme of Action* (12 July 1993) UN Doc A/CONF.157/23, para. 8.

incomplete understanding. This issues a big problem where it cannot answer the question of political intolerance, through its adaption of a very ambiguous notion of democratic participation.

1 The *Refah* principle and democratic theory

After assessing the main foundational benchmarks of the right to democracy in international law, the focus needs to be shifted to the substance of democracy, in order to complement the doctrinal deficiencies with significant judicial decisions and foundational theoretical components. Although – as explained earlier – the substantive understanding of democracy in international law provides a richer and more rigorous comprehension of the term; it certainly is not enough – as it stands – to guarantee a secure application of democratic governance, beyond the threat of intolerant Islamist actors. This is due to a number of reasons. First, the substantive account of democracy in international law does not sufficiently engage with the citizen, who is the first unit of a democratic society, and to whom the right is limited. This is a significant doctrinal problem, where the requirement of reasonableness is essential to guarantee the avoidance of the misuse of free and fair elections.

Second, the substantive account sets out positive obligations on States and actors to whom international law attaches rights and duties. This cannot be efficient, where the issue needs to be addressed from the grassroots (citizens and political actors in the national level). This is the only possible course to establish a democratic society, with all the necessary pillars to avoid the rise of political intolerance, through the establishment of a mature form of popular sovereignty that will guarantee the sustainability of democracy, as a means to secure the protection of other fundamental rights and freedoms. Therefore, there is a consequential requirement for the content of the right to democracy in international law to be richer and more substantive. This needs to be done with reference to the *Refah* principle and the consideration of the fundamental pillars of democracy as provided in traditional and contemporary democratic thought.

Refah Partisi (Welfare Party) and others v Turkey, stands as an example of the importance of supranational judicial supervision on the protection of democracy.[19] Refah Partisi came to power in Turkey in 1995, and its leader

19 *Refah Partisi (Welfare Party) and others v Turkey* (Apps. 41340/98, 41342/98 and 41344/98), Judgment of the Grand Chamber of 13 February 2003.

Erbakan, became the nation's first Islamist prime minister since the fall of the Ottoman Empire. His party was accused of the introduction of Islamization measures to the country in violation of the constitution and the principles of secularism. Turkey's constitutional court suspended the party, and its members appealed to the European Court of Human Rights on the violation of Article 11 of the European Convention of Human Rights (freedom of assembly).[20] The Court concluded that such suspension acted in conformity with the relevant provision in the Convention, and was necessary to sustain democratic governance in the nation.[21]

The Court's verdict is seen to be controversial.[22] It failed to provide an in-depth assessment of the political ideology of Refah. Understanding the philosophical roots of the organization is necessary in order to comprehend its compatibility with democracy. Nonetheless, the *Refah* principle could be defined in the view of this book as: any necessary measure taken by the relevant impartial authorities to impose a limitation on the political activity of a certain intolerant group based on the pillar of reasonableness, with the aim to protect democracy against its enemies. Such measure needs not to be taken by a supranational judicial body, where in this previous example, it was originally initiated by the corresponding nation's constitutional court. However, the question of reasonableness is the most central criteria for the enactment of the previous principle, and thus will be the main focus of this book.

Support for the *Refah* principle could be found in the foundational works of leading traditional and contemporary democratic thinkers. The international

20 Article 11 of the ECHR states:

1 Everyone has the right to freedom of peaceful assembly and to freedom of association with others, including the right to form and to join trade unions for the protection of his interests.
2 No restrictions shall be placed on the exercise of these rights other than such as are prescribed by law and are necessary in a democratic society in the interests of national security or public safety, for the prevention of disorder or crime, for the protection of health or morals or for the protection of the rights and freedoms of others. This article shall not prevent the imposition of lawful restrictions on the exercise of these rights by members of the armed forces, of the police or of the administration of the State.

21 *Refah Partisi (Welfare Party) and others v Turkey* (n 19) paras 98–9 of the judgment.

22 See K Boyle, 'Human Rights, Religion and Democracy: The Refah Partisi Case' (2004) 1 *Essex Human Rights Review* 1; S Langlaude, 'Indoctrination, Secularism, Religious Liberty and the ECHR' (2006) 55 *ICLQ* 929; F Tulkens, 'The European Convention on Human Rights and Church-State Relations: Pluralism vs. Pluralism' (2008) 30 *Cardozo Law Review* 2575.

law democracy norm does share some family resemblance with the idea of democracy that emerged in Western political thought. Democracy is one expression of the social contract theory of legitimate political authority. The classical texts understood legitimate political authority with regard to consent and the role of religion in the political life of the citizen. Secularism was indeed an element of democratic stability in the theory, although it may not be clearly expressed in the texts.

The role of the citizen is central to this book. This is because the right to democracy in international law is a citizen's right. Only citizens practise the right to political participation in the form of *inter alia* the right to stand for elections and the right to vote. The contemporary social contract tradition focuses on the role of the citizen in the *democratic society*.

The political pre-conditions of democracy require an agreement on the role of religion in public life. The work of John Rawls is the best reflection of the social contract in its contemporary perspective, where it provided an illustration of an instrumental right to democracy. This notion encompasses that democracy is to be used as an instrument to achieve a moral objective, which is in this context, liberty. *A Theory of Justice* and *Political Liberalism* describe how a social contract can only be formed between reasonable citizens. This establishes a formula for participation in the democratic process based on the condition of reasonableness.[23] This foundation could be seen as a philosophical interpretation of the *Refah* principle, which introduced a rule to exclude intolerant actors from participation in the democratic process.

The importance of citizenship lies upon the fact that democracy is a citizen's right. Therefore, this leads one to assess whether those who have their own conception of the good, reflected in a comprehensive doctrine which competes with democracy as a form of legitimate government are reasonable, and whether or not they could be parties to a social contract since their conception of the good is not built behind a veil of ignorance. The social contract in its contemporary form introduces a method by which democracy could succeed sustainably as a right on an instrumental foundation; however, is that enough to maintain a human right to democracy? The answer to that question is that it could be seen as a starting point, and one should comprehend that the political evolution of mankind is continuous.

23 J Rawls, *Political Liberalism* (expanded edn, Columbia University Press 1996); *A Theory of Justice* (revised edn, Harvard University Press 1999).

2 Limitations

This book is concerned with a number of doctrinal and theoretical "issues". It is important to emphasize here that the doctrinal section will engage with the right to democracy in international law. The idea of the democratic entitlement – advanced by Thomas Franck – is not central to the research question and the analysis. The concept of democracy in international law is also irrelevant to the main assessment.

In terms of democratic theory, this book will engage with the social contract model in its contemporary sense. The reason why this project affirms the social contract as the best expression of democratic theory is because it absorbs that state of society before and after entering the agreement on democratic governance.

John Rawls is the pioneer of the contemporary social contract. He based his theory on the principles of liberty, opportunities, income and wealth. However, this book is only concerned with the first principle, *liberty*, which is relevant to the research problem and the doctrinal assessment of the right to democracy in international law, where it is the basis for the instrumental account of the notion. Therefore, the analysis will not extend to the impact of social and economic welfare and its relation to the establishment of a democratic society.

3 Structure and methodology

In order to achieve the fullest perspective in assessing the right to democracy in international law and contemporary democratic theory, the book will provide an overview on the given subjects. The objective of the first chapter is to present the content and nature of the right to democracy in international law. Based on Article 38 of the Statute of the ICJ, Chapter 1 will assess the position of the right in question in terms of its reflection of international customary law. This chapter will analyze the traditional customary approach, through the identification of State practice and *opinio juris* in this respect. This will be followed by the assessment of the right to democracy in the context of the UDHR, and the evaluation on whether or not the relevant provision reveals modern international customary law. The assessment of the UDHR will extend to the presentation of the drafting history of the document, with particular focus on Article 21, and the context by which it was adopted. This chapter will analyze in detail the content and scope of the democracy norm in the UDHR, and the limitation of the right to democracy to procedural terms. The chapter will conclude with where the right to democracy stands in this setting.

Chapter 2 will extend the doctrinal assessment to the ICCPR, in order to assess the position of the right to democracy in a significant international convention, given that it is a primary source of international law. It will discuss the merits of the democracy provision (Article 25) of the Covenant, and the jurisprudence of the HRC in that respect. It will critically evaluate the communications and General Comment associated with Article 25 of the Covenant. An assessment will be provided of the role of the Committee, and whether or not it was effective in firming the position of democracy as a concept in international law. The chapter will conclude with how this significant international instrument provides an incomplete understanding of the right to democracy, through limiting the notion to the conduct of free and fair elections on a periodic basis.

Having observed and critically assessed the procedural right to democracy as provided in international and regional benchmarks, the focus of this book will extend to include wider developments in international law. This will be through the consideration of the substantive right to democracy, as provided in a series of international and regional instruments. Chapter 4 will present such developments, through the assessment of a number of relevant declarations and instruments issued by the UN General Assembly, Human Rights Commission and other appropriate regional and international bodies.

The doctrinal section will conclude on a conceptual observation, that international legal instruments view the right to political participation as a procedure of periodic free and fair elections. Although many improvements have been made on this understanding by international and regional bodies, State practice and the conduct of international organizations does not concretely enforce the richer conceptualization of the notion.

The contemporary account of the theory will be presented through evaluating the major works of John Rawls. This is important to the argument since Rawls provides a comprehensive understanding of the citizen, and his/her role in a democratic society. His analysis contributes to affording a wider understanding of fundamental terms associated with democracy, that international law failed to provide, such as the overlapping consensus, public reason, toleration and political pluralism. Rawls's works reflect an instrumental right to democracy, where the notion is to be used to achieve liberty as an end, and cannot be achieved without reasonableness.

Rawls's understanding of the role of the citizen will be the main point of evaluation. The expansion of the view that democracy is more than a right to vote is also of vital importance, through observing other requirements of the establishment of a democratic society, such as toleration, pluralism and political liberalism. The focus of Chapter 5 will be on Rawls's principle of liberty, which is the aim of the instrumental understanding of democracy, and the academic critique and support associated with the aforementioned principle, and the consequences that follow its application in accordance with the Rawlsian model.

1 The right to democracy in international customary law

1.1 Introduction

It is of vital significance to advance the argument that the developing right to democracy in international law should be catalogued into two categories: the procedural right to democracy and the substantive right to the notion. The procedural right, which dominated the international arena, especially during the Cold War era, is based on limiting the concept to periodic free and fair elections. This understanding of the term was fundamentally evident in the context of the Universal Declaration of Human Rights (UDHR) and the International Covenant on Civil and Political Rights (ICCPR).[1] This was due to ideological polarization in the drafting process of each instrument and subsequent State practice that defined the limitations provided in the scope and content of such form of government.

The procedural right to democracy could be described as a citizen's right to free and fair elections on a periodic basis.[2] This incorporates the right to vote and the right to be elected in free and free elections. The Austrian–American economist, Joseph Schumpeter advanced a very unwavering rationale in *Capitalism, Socialism and Democracy* supporting the limitation of the right to the mere procedure of elections.[3] In his view, popular

1 Universal Declaration of Human Rights (adopted 10 December 1948) UNGA Res 217 A (III) UN Doc A/810 (hereinafter UDHR); International Covenant on Civil and Political Rights (adopted 16 December 1966. Entered into force 3 January 1976) UNGA Res 2200A (XXI) UN Doc A/6316 999 UNTS 171; (1967) 6 *ILM* 368 (hereinafter ICCPR).

2 R Burchill, 'The Developing International Law of Democracy' (2001) 64 *Modern Law Review* 123, 125.

3 JA Schumpeter, *Capitalism, Socialism and Democracy* (Harper & Row 1942). It is important to note here that the minimalist democratic view extended in American democratic thought, not limited to Schumpeter's analogy. See generally D Truman, *The Governmental Process* (Knopf 1951); B Berelson, 'Democratic Theory and Public Opinion' (1952) 16 *Public Opinion Quarterly* 313; A Downs, *An Economic Theory of Democracy* (Harper & Row 1957);

democracy should not be embraced, where it could lead to the triumph of Socialism, an ideal that he did not welcome. Instead, in the name of realism, he believed that democracy was a construct to preserve elitist dominance. Therefore, it should be stripped from its entire ethical context.[4]

In terms of ethics, Schumpeter believed that there was no 'will of the people' and common good. This is significant in terms of assessing the notion in the context of international law, especially Article 21 of the UDHR which explicitly states: 'The will of the people shall be the basis of the authority of government.' To Schumpeter, democracy was a leaders' competition for votes, and the competing leaders thereof deliver the will of the people. This minimalist view of the procedural right to democracy cannot be taken into thoughtful account when assessing the context of the term in international law.

A modern post-Cold War evaluation of Schumpeter's theory could find some merit in his argument when assessing the events in the Arab World. The procedural electoral system did lead to the triumph and collapse of intolerant political Islam – in contrast to Socialism – as he advanced. The uprisings in the region were youth-dominated and populist by and large. However, the rationale stipulated in his manifestation cannot be accepted, where the will of the people and common good should be the ultimate guarantees for the sustainability of democracy. Therefore, instead of minimalizing, it should be maximized to include more rights beyond the procedure of elections by incorporating other rights and fundamental freedoms, where democracy becomes an end not a means to reach power. In other words, according to CB Macpherson, 'the egalitarian principle inherent in democracy requires not only "one man, one vote," but also "one man, one equal right to live as fully humanly as he may wish".'[5]

The main objective of this chapter is to illustrate the position of the right to democracy in international customary law. This will be through the assessment of the position of the right in question in traditional international custom, and the modern approach to international declarative law in the context

W Kornhauser, *The Politics of Mass Society* (Free Press 1959); RA Dahl, *Who Governs?* (Yale University Press 1961); G Schubert, *The Public Interest* (Free Press 1962).

4 For a critique on this minimalist view, see generally JL Walker, 'A Critique of the Elitist Theory of Democracy' (1966) 60 *The American Political Science Review* 285; DM Ricci, 'Democracy Attenuated: Schumpeter, the Process Theory and American Democratic Thought' (1970) 32 *The Journal of Politics* 239; G Mackie, 'Schumpeter's Leadership Democracy' (2009) 37 *Political Theory* 128.

5 CB Macpherson, *Democratic Theory* (Clarendon Press 1973) 51 as cited in R Burchill, 'Moving beyond Markets and Minimalism: Democracy in the Era of Globalization' (2008) 8 *Human Rights & Human Welfare* 17, 27.

of the UDHR, as provided by leading academic analysis. This chapter will then assess the merits of the right to democracy as provided in Article 21 of the Declaration. It will provide how the right in this context is procedural in its nature, and the application of the procedural right to democracy is insufficient, especially in the context of the Arab World. The thin electoral model cannot provide the necessary guarantees to maintain democracy in a sustained fashion, particularly in transitional societies. International law needs to be an instrument to empower individuals. However, when solely applying the minimalist procedural element of the right to democracy, it becomes a tool that implements unequal power relations between those who are prescribed as equal individuals.[6] This is therefore a significant conceptual problem, which requires an in-depth assessment. Understanding the right to democracy in the context of the UDHR is significant to the analysis, since it is the first international instrument to recognize the term as a human right. The evaluation of the right to democracy in this context will conclude on a reflection and critique on where it stands in international customary law and in the most significant human rights instrument.

1.2 The right to democracy in traditional international customary law

Article 38 of the Statute of the International Court of Justice (ICJ) stated that international custom is one of the primary sources of international law. International custom is determined by State practice accompanied by *opinio juris*. The identification of international customary law – in its traditional sense – is based on a number of elements as advanced by Manley Hudson. First, the coherent practice by a number of States. This has to be with respect to a precise subject in international relations (including human rights). Second, the frequency of such practice over a considerable period of time. Third, the general understanding that such practice is prescribed by international law. And, finally, the common harmony in the practice with other States that confirmed such norm.[7]

From the above definition and outline, the recognition of traditional customary international law with respect to the subject of this chapter will be based on the criteria of generality and acceptance as law.[8] The ICJ in the

6 Burchill, ibid 26.
7 FL Kirgis Jr., 'Custom in a Sliding Scale' (1987) 81 *AJIL* 146.
8 IC MacGibbon, 'Customary International Law and Acquiescence' (1957) 33 *British Yearbook of International Law* 115, 117, 121.

Fisheries Jurisdiction Cases affirmed the principle of generality.[9] The generality criterion encompasses the acceptance of a legal norm by a significant number of States.[10] Silence could imply in this case either tacit acceptance or non-interest.[11]

The second principle is 'acceptance as law' which was upheld by the ICJ in the *Continental Shelf Cases*.[12] The Court provided: 'There are many international acts, e.g. in the field of ceremonial and protocol, which are performed almost invariably, but which are motivated only by considerations of courtesy, convenience or tradition and not by any sense of legal duty.'[13] It is important to note here that, unlike international treaties, where the determination of an international law norm and State obligation is straightforward, the recognition of international custom could be harder to identify.[14]

However, from the above elements of international customary law, one could conclude that there is no positive State practice accompanied by *opinio juris* with regard to the right to democracy for a number of reasons. First, if State practice confirmed the right to democracy in international law as an international customary norm, then the non-application of democratic governance would be seen as a violation of international law. This is certainly not the case, where the international community issued positive measures against States for the violation of other fundamental rights of freedoms that did not coherently extend to the right to democracy.[15]

Second, State practice did not demonstrate a clear affirmation of democracy as a form of government. The international community has seen a rise in non-democratic superpowers, without any serious objection. This was in contrast to the consistent and firm international condemnation of fascism

9 *Fisheries Jurisdiction Case (Federal Republic of Germany v Iceland)* (Merits) [1973] ICJ Rep 56. For more on this, see generally C Hudson, 'Fisheries and Economic Zones as Customary International Law' (1980) 70 *San Diego Law Review* 661.

10 MacGibbon (n 8) 117–8.

11 H Kelsen, *Principles of International Law* (The Lawbook Exchange 1952) 361.

12 *North Sea Continental Shelf Cases (Federal Republic of Germany v Denmark; Federal Republic of Germany v Netherlands)* (Merits) [1969] ICJ Rep 52.

13 Ibid para. 77. The judgment of the ICJ caused come controversy in this case, where the aforementioned principle was criticized. See W Friedmann, 'North Sea Continental Cases – A Critique' (1970) 64 *AJIL* 229.

14 P Allot, 'Language, Method and the Nature of International Law' (1971) 45 *British Yearbook of International Law* 103, 129.

15 S Murphy, 'Democratic Legitimacy and the Recognition of States and Governments' in GH Fox and BR Roth (eds), *Democratic Governance in International Law* (Cambridge University Press 2000) 123, 128; S Wheatley, 'Democracy in International Law: A European Perspective' (2002) 51 *ICLQ* 225, 233.

and apartheid as forms of government. This shows that there is no international commitment to democracy as a human right.[16]

Further, the right to democracy does not exist in traditional international custom because the concept of pro-democratic military intervention is not supported by State practice and international organizations.[17] The notion of pro-democracy regime change was condemned by the General Assembly on many occasions, and is a controversial issue in international law.[18] Therefore, if there were an international binding customary norm in this respect, the aforementioned concept would have been accepted as a necessary action.

From the above, one could safely assert that there is no international customary norm on the right to democracy in international law. This was through the assessment of the traditional approach to international customary law. However, the observation of the wider understanding of this source requires the consideration of the modern customary approach as provided in the context of the UDHR.

1.3 The right to democracy in modern international customary law: the Universal Declaration of Human Rights

The UDHR is mainly the first fundamental international document to mildly recognize democracy as a concept in international law. It instituted the foundations of a new human rights order that gave the meaning of humanity a new understanding. The UNGA adopted the UDHR on 10 December 1948 with 48 votes in favour, eight abstentions and none against. This demonstrates how the newly founded international community at the time took the issue of human rights seriously. The Chairperson of the Human Rights Commission, Eleanor Roosevelt, who drafted the Declaration, proclaimed its significance, considering it 'the Magna Carta of all mankind'.[19]

The UDHR, together with the ICCPR and the International Covenant on Economic, Social and Cultural rights comprise the International Bill of Human Rights. However, the Declaration is the foundation of the codification

16 J d'Aspremont, 'The Rise and Fall of Democracy Governance in International Law: A Reply to Susan Marks' (2011) 22 *EJIL* 549, 551

17 GH Fox and BR Roth, 'Democracy in International Law' (2001) 27 *Review of International Studies* 327, 339.

18 See M Byers and S Chesterman, '"You the People": Pro-Democratic Intervention in International Law' in GH Fox and BR Roth (eds), *Democratic Governance in International Law* (Cambridge University Press 2000) 259.

19 H Lauterpacht, *International Law and Human Rights* (Stevens 1950) 146.

of modern human rights, and the most universal and comprehensive international document in that respect. Therefore, it stands today as a first reference to human rights and 'the single most cited human rights instrument'.[20]

The UDHR covered a wide range of rights. Civil, political, economic, cultural and social rights were protected by the Declaration, which makes it a very comprehensive human rights document. This led some commentators to consider the comprehensive codification of rights in its context as modern international customary law.[21] The modern declarative approach to international customary law will be the beginning point of the analysis. A conclusion on the position of the right to democracy in the context of binding international law is necessary to comprehend the compelling position of the notion. The focus of this section will then extend to the merits of Article 21 of the Declaration. This will be achieved through providing a detailed presentation of the drafting history of the UDHR, especially in the context of the democracy provision. The importance of engaging with the *travaux préparatoires* of the Declaration is necessary in order to comprehend the political and historic conditions that led to the adoption of the right to democracy in this procedural context. They are furthermore important since the observance of the drafting history is to a very high extent explanatory to the text. This section will also present a detailed assessment of the merits of Article 21, in terms of its encompassment of a procedural understanding of democracy, which does not extend beyond the right to free and fair elections on a periodic basis.

a The legal value of the Universal Declaration of Human Rights

In order to assess the merits of the provision on the right to political participation, one must first briefly bring to the discussion the longstanding academic debate on the legal value of the UDHR in order to have an appropriate understanding whether or not this document has a binding status and, thus, understand the position of democracy in its context. At first, both States and commentators considered the Declaration as a soft law instrument that lacked any binding status and only set out a common language amongst the members of the UN in addressing the issue

20 HJ Steiner, P Alston and R Goodman, *International Human Rights in Context: Law, Politics, Morals* (3rd edn, Oxford University Press 2008) 136.

21 See AE Roberts, 'Traditional and Modern Approaches to Customary International Law: A Reconciliation' (2001) 95 *AJIL* 757.

of human rights.[22] However, this argument is not accepted in this stage where State practice provided otherwise, in terms of some fundamental rights at least. Today there is something of an academic consensus that the Declaration is a binding legal document, in terms of some of the rights it covers, however, there is a wide debate on under which grounds do some provisions in this instruments find their binding character. This debate will be presented in some detail in this section.

The Charter of the UN made brief reference to human rights; though it failed to address them in detail. The post-Second World War era needed to emphasize the issue of human rights, in order to avoid wide-spread mass violations that occurred on mankind, and also to avoid the failure of the newly established international organization, the UN, to protect fundamental human rights as happened to its predecessor, the League of Nations.

Since the Declaration was adopted only three years after the establishment of the UN in 1945, this led some to consider it as 'an authoritative interpretation of the Charter'.[23] Therefore, it is a binding international instrument 'in its own right' which reflects the international community's position on the issue of human rights.[24] This argument was supported by a number of State representatives, including the representative of Chile who asserted: 'violations by any State of the rights enumerated in the Declaration would mean violation of the principles of the United Nations'.[25]

In assessing this approach, one may observe that it is important to consider the Declaration as an authoritative interpretation of the Charter of the United Nations, not only because this makes it a legally binding instrument, but also to avoid any inconsistency in its interpretations by States since such inconsistence would preclude a truly universal consensus about human rights. However, this assertion cannot be accepted, where State practice does

22 See for example J Goldsmith, 'Should International Human Rights Law Trump US Domestic Law?' (2000) 1 *Chicago Journal of International Law* 327, 335–8; D Cassel, 'Does International Human Rights Law Make a Difference?' (2001) 2 *Chicago Journal of International Law* 121, 135; OA Hathaway, 'Do Human Rights Treaties Make a Difference?' (2002) 111 *Yale Law Journal* 1935, 2023. Also, a number of States challenged the binding status of the UDHR when it was first adopted such as: India, Norway, Belorussia, Honduras, Czechoslovakia, Poland, Saudi Arabia, Ukraine and South Africa. See H Lauterpacht, 'The Universal Declaration of Human Rights' (1948) 25 *British Yearbook of International Law* 354, 356–65.

23 LB Sohn, 'The Human Rights Law of the Charter' (1977) 12 *Texas International Law Journal* 129, 133.

24 Ibid.

25 UN Doc A/C.3/SR. 91 at 97, as cited in J Rehman, *International Human Rights Law* (2nd edn, Longman 2010) 80.

not support such legal classification, nor was there enough commitment by State representatives – other than Chile – to such approach.

Other commentators assert that the UDHR reflects traditional international customary law.[26] In order to accept a given norm as international customary law, State practice has to be evident and accompanied by *opinio juris*.[27] According to Brownlie, proof of State practice could be evident through a long list of sources including 'diplomatic correspondence, policy statements, press releases, the opinions of official legal advisors . . . state legislation, international and national judicial decisions, recitals in treaties and other international instruments, a pattern of treaties in the same form, the practice of international organs, and resolutions relating to legal questions in the United Nations General Assembly'.[28] Any of these sources prove that State practice is strongly evident; with regard to the UDHR it will be elaborated on further in this assessment. Moreover, others add to Brownlie's list that evidence for State practice with regard to the UDHR is found in many national constitutions that had direct reference to the Declaration.[29] All of these factors show that the UDHR reflects international customary law. However, again, this approach cannot be accepted when applying to the Declaration as a whole, where State practice provides minimal to no commitment to some of the provisions of the Declaration, including, the right to democracy.

Some commentators have provided an alternative 'modern' understanding of international customary law. According to Roberts, international custom is developed through 'general statements of rules' instead of traditional State practice and, therefore, through a deductive process.[30] Modern custom may be developed by international organizations such as the UN through

26 See for example JP Humphrey, *No Distant Millennium: The International Law of Human Rights* (UNESCO 1989) 155; P Thornberry, *International Law and the Rights of Minorities* (Clarendon Press 1991) 238; H Hannum, 'The Status of the Universal Declaration of Human Rights in National and International Law' (1995/6) 25 *Georgia Journal of International and Comparative Law* 287, 317.

27 For more about international customary law, see JL Kunz, 'The Nature of Customary International Law' (1953) 47 *AJIL* 662; H Lauterpacht, *The Development of International Law by the International Court* (Stevens 1958); AA D'Amato, *The Concept of Custom in International Law* (Cornell University Press 1971).

28 I Brownlie, *Principles of Public International Law* (4th edn, Oxford University Press 1990) 5, as cited in Hannum (n 26) 320.

29 O Schachter, *International Law in Theory and Practice* (Martinus Nijhoff 1991) 336. Many national constitutions have direct reference to the UDHR, such as the constitutions of Afghanistan (1990), Cambodia (1993), Chad (1993) and Comoros (1992). See Hannum (n 26) 355.

30 Roberts (n 21) 758.

its General Assembly, which might easily establish new customs or declare existing ones.[31] When Roberts's modern approach is applied, the right to democracy and political participation will be more evident than relying on traditional State practice and *opinio juris*. The reason behind this is that it will be difficult to set an international standard of democratic governance that will be accepted and practised by States. Also, it will take a long period to prove the element of *opinio juris*. Therefore, at least with regard to international human rights, and especially the right to democracy and political participation, the international community should take the modern custom approach into consideration, in order to achieve better outcomes to fundamental human rights.

On the other hand, Chodosh rejects Roberts's approach of classifying declarations as international custom.[32] His rejection is based on the Statute of the International Court of Justice which defines international custom as 'general practice accepted as law'.[33] According to this provision, declarations cannot be categorized as international customary law. Therefore, Chodosh asserts that there must be no confusion between international customary law and 'international declarative law', since both are different in terms of their source and nature.[34]

However, the difference between international declarative law and modern customary law is superficial. Although it may be argued that the source of each one is different, the result is nonetheless the same. Both lead to binding effects on States without the formalities of traditional international customary law of State practice and *opinio juris*. Therefore, the debate on whether or not international declarative law is in fact much different from modern customary law is indeed very technical and does not lead to a fruitful conclusion.

Other scholars consider that it is the fact that the UDHR is firmly established in international law that gives it a *jus cogens* character.[35] This approach lacks consensus since the international community is not yet ready to be obliged to all of the provisions of the Declarations. However, some of the rights protected by the Declaration might have a *jus cogens* character,

31 Ibid.

32 HE Chodosh, 'Neither Treaty Nor Custom: The Emergence of Declarative International Law' (1991) 26 *Texas International Law Journal* 87, 88. Other commentators also have reference to declarative international law, see D Bodansky, 'Customary (and not so Customary) International Environmental Law' (1995) 3 *Symposium: International Environmental Laws and Agencies: The Next Generation* 105.

33 Article 38 of the Statute of the ICJ.

34 Chodosh (n 34) 89.

35 J Rehman, *International Human Rights Law* (2nd edn., Longman 2009) 86.

such as the right to equality (Article 1), freedom from slavery (Article 4) and freedom from torture and other cruel or inhuman or degrading treatment (Article 5).

Nonetheless, with regard to the binding status of Article 21 (right to democracy) on the basis of its reflection of international customary law in its modern account, the conclusion could solely be based on State practice in that respect. The observation of State practice with regard to the binding status of Article 21 of the Declaration does not confirm a commitment to a right to democracy. This is based on the reasons mentioned earlier in this chapter in the analysis of the traditional customary law approach, regarding the rise of international super-powers, the condemnation of pro-democracy military intervention, and, the international community's lack of collective enforcing measures on violations to the right in question. Also, another specific reason applies to the dismissal of the international customary approach in the context of the UDHR. The relevant provision in the Declaration provided no specific procedures or guidelines for the establishment of an electoral system in a particular political setting.[36] Therefore, it is not possible to recognize State practice in that respect with the lack of the specifics necessary for identification. The vagueness and ambiguity of Article 21 of the UDHR makes it very difficult to determine the details necessary for an accurate identification of State practice. Therefore, in both traditional and modern approaches, the right to democracy does not reflect international customary law.

b Article 21: between **travaux préparatoires** *and substance*

Having observed the legal value of the UDHR, and how the right to democracy in its context does not reflect modern international customary law, it is important to observe the content of Article 21, which was the first significant provision to recognize a right to democracy in international law. The consideration of the drafting history is necessary to comprehend the setting by which the provision was adopted. The General Assembly approved the establishment of the Commission on Human Rights upon the recommendation of the Economic and Social Council (ECOSOC) in 1946. The main task of the Commission was to draft an international bill of rights. The Commission included some distinguished members such as René Cassin and Charles Malik, and was chaired by Eleanor Roosevelt. The General Assembly's Humanitarian and Cultural Committee (Third Committee) and

36 Wheatley (n 15) 238.

Legal Committee (Sixth Committee) have also had a significant role in the deliberations in the drafting process of the Declaration.[37]

The UDHR covered all aspects of what is known today as the first generation of human rights, including economic and social rights in addition to political and civil rights. Although the international community was in the midst of an ideological conflict in light of the Cold War, the right to political participation was included in the UDHR. Article 21 of the Declaration provided:

> (1) Everyone has the right to take part in the government of his country, directly or through freely chosen representatives.
> (2) Everyone has the right of equal access to public service in his country.
> (3) The will of the people shall be the basis of the authority of government; this will shall be expressed in periodic and genuine elections which shall be by universal and equal suffrage and shall be held by secret vote or by equivalent free voting procedures.

The drafting history of this provision is rather interesting and very interpretive. Mrs Newland, the representative of New Zealand in the Third Committee considered the Article as 'one of the most important in the declaration'.[38] Of course, that position was taken in an era that witnessed the beginning of the Cold War and ideological tensions that were clearly evident in the discussions on the draft Declaration in the Third Committee.

The Belgian delegation stressed political pluralism through an emphasis on the multi-party system in the Third Committee's 134th meeting. The Soviet representative, Mr Pavlov, strongly rejected the Belgian statement, on the grounds that 'the bourgeois class had ceased to exist' in the Soviet Union, and that the Communist Party was capable on its own in looking after the interests of workers and peasants in its territory.[39]

In terms of substance, the term 'everyone' was discussed by delegates which resulted in its replacement with 'every citizen'.[40] This came from a standpoint that the right to political participation was to be limited to citizens only, which should have been considered by the Commission in order to avoid any ambiguity. It could also be seen that 'everyone' in his or her

37 See generally, WA Schabas, *The Universal Declaration of Human Rights: The Travaux Préparatoires* (Cambridge University Press 2013).

38 UN Doc A/C.3/SR. 133.

39 UN Doc A/C.3/SR. 134.

40 UN Doc A/C.3/SR. 133.

nation was to practise the rights covered in Article 21. However, the term shows some ambiguity, where it could be extended to minors and others with legal disabilities.

The UDHR was clearly influenced by the French Declaration of the Rights of Man and of Citizen (1789).[41] Though it largely came as a response to certain historical conditions following the events of the Second World War, the Declaration maintained a lot of principles covered by the 1789 text. In terms of its style, the UDHR had a sense of antiquity and reference to the Enlightenment and natural law.[42] According to Stephen Marks, the principles of the French Revolution as echoed in the Declaration of the Rights of Man and of Citizen and other theoretical essays have roots in antiquity and ancient philosophical texts.[43] However, French enlightenment philosophy strongly supported individual autonomy over communal collectivism.[44] This is indeed evident in the spirit of the UDHR and led the Soviet representative, Mr Bogomolov, to assert that the Declaration was influenced by either the 'French materialist philosophers of the XVIIth century or the New Testament'.[45]

Paragraph (3) caused some controversy amongst the Third Committee. The delegation of the United States abstained from voting on the paragraph because their representative found it encompassing a 'political principle rather than a human right, a theoretical concept rather than a human concept'.[46] The objection is clearly based on 'the will of the people shall be the basis of the authority'. Again, this only shows how the Declaration was influenced by earlier philosophical texts with a sense of antiquity and French romanticism.[47]

Nonetheless, the drafting history fails to address the fact that the Declaration was adopted well before the decolonization era. Most of the nations of sub-Saharan Africa and many parts of the Middle East and Asia had no role

41 Declaration of the Rights of Man and of Citizen, 26 Aug. 1789 (1789), *reprinted in French in* Stéphane Rials, *La Déclaration des droits de l'homme et du citoyen* 21–6 (1988), *reprinted in English in* George A. Berman, Henry P. de Vries & Nina M. Galston, *French Law: Constitution and Selective Legislation* § 2, at 3 (1994) as cited in SP Marks, 'From the "Single Confused Page" to the "Decalogue for Six Billion Persons": The Roots of the Universal Declaration of Human Rights in the French Revolution' (1998) 20 *HRQ* 459.

42 Marks, ibid 471–80.

43 Ibid 471.

44 Ibid 474.

45 A Verdoodt, *Naissance et Signification de la Déclaration Universelle des Droits de l'Homme* (1964) 79–80 as cited in Marks, ibid 490.

46 UN Doc A/C.3/SR. 134.

47 For more on the French influence on the UDHR, see J Henkin, 'Rights: Here and There' (1981) 81 *Columbia Law Review* 1592, 1597.

in drafting the UDHR. The universal approach of the Declaration revealed Western (French) idealism, especially with respect to the right to political participation, not to mention an ideological polarization between Soviet and liberal democratic camps. However, the practice of decolonized nations reflected afterwards their commitment to the Declaration and to the international human rights regime.

Article 21 covered the main aspects of political participation as provided earlier. It viewed the right to political participation as an entitlement; and yet, it failed to make reference to pluralism, secularism or even the term 'democracy'. However, it Article 21 cannot be understood nor applied without taking Article 29(2) into account, which stated that 'in the exercise of his rights and freedoms, everyone shall be subject only to such limitations as are determined by law solely for the purpose of securing due recognition and respect for the rights and freedoms of others and of meeting the just requirements of morality, public order and the general welfare in a democratic society'. This is a compelling statement that certainly shows a commitment to democracy and enriches the right to political participation in the UDHR.[48] However, such reference to the term *democracy* should have been in the text of Article 21 itself, in order to reaffirm that the right to political participation is echoed in democracy as a form of government. It is therefore difficult to comprehend the establishment of a democratic society in a non-democratic polity, and political stagnation in the drafting process resulted nonetheless in the lacking of a coherent assurance of democracy as an entitlement.

1.4 A monitoring mechanism?

In 1956, the ECOSOC introduced a periodic reporting mechanism under Article 64 of the UN Charter.[49] States were to submit a periodic report regarding their implementation of the rights covered by the UDHR once every three years to the Commission on Human Rights.[50] The step seemed to be a revolutionary one, that could have ensured the universal protection of human rights and given the Declaration an unquestionable mandatory status as early as the 1950s. However, according to Humphrey – who was one of the main drafters of the UDHR – the idea was ineffective, due to the

48 HJ Steiner, 'Political Participation as a Human Right' (1988) 1 *Harvard Human Rights Yearbook* 77, 88–9.

49 JP Humphrey, 'The International Bill of Rights: Scope and Implementation' (1976) 17 *William and Mary Law Review* 527, 529–30.

50 Ibid 530.

'political considerations' of the Commission, the lack of effective individual communication system and, most of all, the absence of State cooperation in many cases.[51]

The reporting mechanism was modified in 1970, under ECOSOC Resolution 1503, which created a procedure for individual communications on violations of human rights.[52] The violations were not limited to the rights covered in the UDHR, and the procedure was extended to all States, even those that were not members in the UN. The 1503 procedure was adopted in 1970, and continued until the establishment of the new international human rights regime in 2006, where the Human Rights Council replaced the Commission.[53]

However, although the 1503 procedure looked theoretically a compelling one, it certainly failed and proved to be ineffective with many shortcomings. The reason behind this was the confidential nature of the communication system.[54] This, in addition to the political considerations of the Commission, led the international community to establish a new international human rights regime, where the Human Rights Council replaced the Commission, and the adoption of a more effective individual communication mechanism within the Council; not to mention, the Universal Periodic Review mechanism, which proved to be a very effective tool in the protection of international human rights.

Therefore, it is safe to say that the UDHR lacked an effective enforcement mechanism because it was not intended to be a self-executing instrument. The 1503 procedure was an introductory instrument, in the evolving international human rights regime. It was certainly not an effective one, but – like the Declaration itself – was a foundation for the establishment of more detailed and operational instruments. Further, the individual communication system was not solely based on the UDHR and, thus, it could not be seen exclusively as the Declaration's enforcement instrument. However, with regard to the right to democracy in the context of the Declaration, the failure of the 1503 procedure to be an enforcement and subsequently an interpretive mechanism, led to the enhancement of the minimalist understanding of the right in question, where it could have been redefined by international practice to include more mutually reinforcing rights in order to speed up the development of the international law of democracy.

51 Ibid 532.

52 ECOSOC Res 1503 (XLVIII) (adopted 27 May 1970) UN Doc E/4832/Add.1.

53 For a detailed assessment, see C Callejon, 'Developments at the Human Rights Council in 2007: A Reflection of Its Ambivalence' (2008) 8 *Human Rights Law Review* 323, 331–4.

54 Ibid 332–3; ME Tardu, 'United Nations Response to Gross Violations of Human Rights: The 1503 Procedure' (1980) 20 *Santa Carla Law Review* 559, 598–9.

1.5 Conclusion

The examination of State practice accompanied by *opinio juris* provided that the right to democracy does not reflect international customary law in its traditional understanding. The position of the right in question in the UDHR also demonstrates that it does not mirror modern international custom. This assertion is not only justified by the lack of State practice for reasons mentioned earlier, but also, the difficulty to determine the nature and content of the notion, as provided in the vague wording of Article 21 of the Declaration. The lack of such elaboration on key terms such as 'genuine elections' is an ambiguity that cannot be a definite source of reference. In other words, the vagueness of the terms associated with the right in question is problematic, and State practice cannot be determined on an uncertain provision.

However, one must acknowledge that Article 21 of the Declaration provided the first codification of a right to democracy in international law. The provision delivered a basic design for a right to democracy. It failed to engage in detail with the definition, nature and scope of the concept. Democracy is a very wide term that could have many interpretations. The following observations are necessary to fully comprehend the position of the right to democracy in the UDHR.

Article 21 of the Declaration failed to incorporate the term *democracy* in its text. As provided earlier in the drafting process of the Declaration, political polarization from the Cold War was a main reason to this, and was central to such limitation. The failure to explicitly have reference to the notion undermines the content of the provision in terms of its commitment to democratic governance.

The failure of the 1503 procedure on the other hand to be an effective monitoring and interpreting mechanism only added to the uncertainty associated with the provision. Where there has been an effective monitoring body with the Declaration, an extended conclusion could have been reached on the merits of the relevant article based on jurisprudence and individual communications. However, this is certainly not the case in the UDHR.

Further, 'The will of the people' has been linked to elections as provided in the text of Article 21. This affirms that the commitment under this provision is a procedural one. Although it could be interpreted that such popular will could vote standing regimes out of power through *genuine* elections, it still encompasses a minimalist view.[55] This study does not suggest that the

55 GH Fox and B Roth, 'Democracy and International Law' (2001) 27 *Review of International Studies* 327, 336.

wording of Article 21 was intended to accommodate Schumpeter's view on procedural democracy; however, due to political considerations and historical reasons the content of the article certainly did not provide a comprehensive substantive view of democracy. The failure of Article 21 to address the main pillars of democracy, such as pluralism, reasonableness and public reasoning in order to satisfy ideological considerations within the international community, is indeed very problematic, where it limits the notion to very abstracted terms. This embraces a very narrow understanding of democracy as the conduct of election on a periodic basis, without the mere reference to at least a multi-party system.

Events in the Arab World show that this understanding is insufficient, and that the thin electoral model cannot succeed in a sustainable fashion. Therefore, going back to Eleanor Roosevelt's statement, one may conclude that the Declaration is indeed a 'Magna Carta of all mankind', however not entirely in terms of the right to democracy. Therefore, the observation of other sources of international law requires the consideration of the position of the right to democracy in the context of international conventions.

2 The right to democracy in international conventions – the International Covenant on Civil and Political Rights

2.1 Introduction

Democracy was established for the first time as a concept in international law, however vaguely, in the UDHR. The failure of the Declaration to acquire an effective monitoring and interpretation mechanism was without doubt an obstacle in properly promoting the value of democracy. This led the international community to look for another effective instrument to promote democracy and political rights.

The international community was committed to establishing a comprehensive international treaty concerned with the protection of fundamental human rights. Through the ECOSOC, the UN General Assembly requested the Human Rights Commission to draft such document.[1] However, it was impossible to make a single document for various political reasons; therefore, it was decided to split it into two: the first concerned with civil and political rights and the second with economic, social and cultural rights.[2] The General Assembly adopted the ICCPR as a comprehensive binding international treaty with regard to political and civil rights in December 1966.[3] The Covenant covered a wide range of rights, such as the right to self-determination (Article 1), the right to life (Article 6), freedom from slavery and the slave trade (Article 8), the right to a fair

1 See P Ghandi, *The Human Rights Committee and the Right of Individual Communication: Law and Practice* (Ashgate 1998) 3; J Rehman, *International Human Rights Law* (2nd edn, Longman 2010) 86.

2 See V Pechota, 'The Development of the Covenant on Civil and Political Rights' in L Henkin (ed.), *The International Bill of Rights: The Covenant on Civil and Political Rights* (Colombia University Press 1981) 32–71.

3 International Covenant on Civil and Political Rights (adopted 16 December 1966. Entered into force 3 January 1976) UNGA Res 2200A (XXI) UN Doc A/6316 999 UNTS 171; (1967) 6 *ILM* 368 (hereinafter ICCPR).

trial (Article 14), the right to peaceful assembly (Article 21) and – the focus of this book – political rights (Article 25). It is indeed one of the most significant international documents with regard to the protection of fundamental human rights.[4]

Having observed the position of the right to democracy in international customary law – in its traditional and modern understandings – in the foregoing chapter, where no international customary norm was identified in this respect, this chapter will extend the doctrinal assessment to include the evaluation of the position of the notion in international conventions, which is another primary source of international law as provided in Article 38 of the Statute of the ICJ. This chapter is focused on the ICCPR, given that it is an important international treaty that covered the right to political participation and the second significant international instrument that limited the definition of the right to democracy in international law to procedural terms. This chapter will therefore begin by presenting a general overview of the Covenant and its drafting history. It will focus on the differences between the ICCPR and the UDHR in terms of its scope, content and the method by which each instrument was adopted. It will then discuss with critique the derogations provided in the Covenant and how they affect the right to political participation. This will be followed by a detailed assessment on the Human Rights Committee (HRC) and its role as the monitoring body of the ICCPR. The focus will be on its general comments function, and its significance to the interpretation of the provisions of the Covenant, especially Article 25. A detailed critical assessment will follow on the right to free and fair elections as provided in the text of the Covenant, the relevant general comment and the HRC's jurisprudence, in the context of its consideration of individual communications and State reports.

The main objective of this chapter is to provide an illustration of the procedural coverage of the right to democracy the context of Article 25 of the ICCPR, where it also encompasses the minimalist view provided in the UDHR, through the limitation of the right to democracy to the procedure of periodic free and fair elections.

4 For more, see generally L Henkin (ed.), *The International Bill of Rights: The Covenant on Civil and Political Rights* (Colombia University Press 1981); D McGoldrick, *The Human Rights Committee: Its Role in the Development of the International Covenant on Civil and Political Rights* (Clarendon Press 1994); M Nowak, *UN Covenant on Civil and Political Rights: CCPR Commentary* (2nd revised edn, NP Engel 2005); HJ Steiner, P Alston and R Goodman, *International Human Rights in Context: Law, Politics, Morals* (3rd edn, Oxford University Press 2008) 151–224.

2.2 Context, background and derogations

The ICCPR is very similar to the UDHR in terms of the rights covered in both documents. The two documents are also similar in the sense that they both aspire to universality.[5] However, on evaluating both instruments, one can find that they are distinctive. First, unlike the UDHR, the Covenant did not afford protection of the right to property.[6] The reason behind this perhaps is that the Covenant is only concerned with civil and political rights that do not basically cover the right to property. Second, the UDHR is a declaration that is not meant to be self-executing and thus does not have an established monitoring body, unlike the ICCPR's Human Rights Committee which is in charge of monitoring the rights protected by the Covenant, and imposes formal obligations on State parties.[7] Therefore, the two instruments are significantly different, although both of them are engaged with the protection of human rights on a universal premise.

The General Assembly recognized the importance of the protection of human rights as early as 1950 by assigning the Human Rights Commission to draft a single comprehensive convention in that respect.[8] The following year, the General Assembly requested that the Commission draft two conventions instead, each based on a different set of rights.[9] The Third Committee reviewed the two drafts of the Human Rights Commission in the years between 1954 and 1966, and the two remaining pillars of the International Bill of Rights were finally adopted on December 1966 by 66 votes to 2 with the abstention of the whole of the Socialist Bloc.[10]

In terms of its interpretation, the HRC applies the Vienna Convention on the Law of Treaties (VCLT) general rules of interpretation. However, human rights instruments are generally illustrated as vague and abstract.[11] Therefore, a liberal interpretation of texts is necessary in the sense that widens the rights covered and limits the restrictions and derogations in order to maintain the purpose of such instruments.[12]

Moreover, the ICCPR seems to find its weakness in its derogation clause. Article 4 of the Covenant provides: 'In time of public emergency which

5 Steiner (n 4) 152.

6 Article 17 of the UDHR provides: '(1) Everyone has the right to own property alone as well as in association with others. (2) No one shall be arbitrarily deprived of his property.' See Rehman (n 1) 86.

7 Rehman, ibid.

8 UNGA Res 421 (V) (4 December 1950).

9 UNGA Res 543 (VI) (5 February 1952).

10 UNGA Res 2200/A (XXI) (16 December 1966) UN Doc A/Res/21/2200.

11 Nowak (n 4) XXVI.

12 Ibid XXVII.

threatens the life of the nation and the existence of which is officially proclaimed, the States Parties to the present Covenant may take measures derogating from their obligations under the present Covenant. . . .' Although the Article prohibited derogation from a number of rights protected by the Covenant, it is still a shortcoming in the protection of international human rights, especially the right to democracy.[13] Such clause, which came with general terms, provides wide discretion to State parties in order to violate the provisions of the ICCPR.[14] In this respect, Meron asserted that: 'The real value of human rights instruments should therefore be tested by examining their derogation clauses.'[15] However, for practical reasons, and in order to *market* the Covenant on the international level, such derogation clause was deemed to be necessary. The reason behind this falls upon the necessity to implement civil and political rights all over the world, but on a gradual basis. Without this clause, many nations would have refused to ratify the ICCPR, and the Covenant would have become a failure. Nevertheless, the drafters should have added Article 25 to the exceptions from which derogations might not be acceptable.

Further, the derogations in Article 4 are not similar to those in Article 29 of the UDHR. The reason behind this is that the Declaration stipulated clearly – as mentioned earlier – that limitations on the rights covered in its text are determined for securing *inter alia* 'the general welfare in a democratic society'. Therefore, such reference provides reassurance for the protection of the right to democracy through the emphasis on the democratic society that is the foundation of democratic governance.

Moreover, the issue of such derogations is all the more problematic since the HRC jurisprudence does not provide conclusive interpretation of the vague terms in Article 4.[16] The term 'state of emergency' is indeed a very vague one, and should not be used by States as an excuse to escape from their international obligations under the Covenant.[17] Therefore, in the absence of compelling interpretation, the issue of derogations remains as one of the most significant weaknesses of the ICCPR, which does not contribute in the

13 Paragraph (2) provided: 'No derogation from articles 6, 7, 8 (paragraphs I and 2), 11, 15, 16 and 18 may be made under this provision.'

14 T Meron, *Human Rights Law-Making in the United Nations: A Critique of Instruments and Process* (Clarendon Press 1986) 87.

15 Ibid.

16 Some reference to the derogations was provided in General Comments 24 and 28.

17 The problem arises when States tend to enact a systematic state of emergency for a long period of time. See for example A Mizok, 'The Legality of the Fifty-Two Year State of Emergency in Israel' (2001) 7 *University of California Davis Journal of International Law and Policy* 223.

establishment of a comprehensive substantive understanding to the right to democracy in international law.

2.3 The Human Rights Committee

Part IV of the ICCPR provided the setting and establishment of the HRC. The HRC is the body in charge of the implementation and monitoring of the ICCPR, and consists of a number of experts in the field of human rights, with high moral standards.[18] HRC consists of 18 elected members who carry out the functions provided in the Covenant,[19] and, act on their own capacity for a four-year term.[20] In other words, they do not act as government representatives. However, these members are eligible for re-election if re-nominated by their States,[21] which is problematic, since States usually keep in mind political considerations when voting for members in human right-monitoring bodies. Another problematic issue will be that although the HRC is a treaty-based monitoring body, it is not totally independent from the United Nations supervision. It is financed from the United Nations, and is subject to the various constraints imposed on all organs under the umbrella of the UN.[22]

Moreover, the leading role of the UN Secretary-General in the process of electing the members of the HRC undermines the Committee's independence,[23] not to mention his important role in circulating information regarding ratification of the ICCPR and its Optional Protocol.[24] All of these factors nevertheless undermine the HRC's independence as a treaty-based human rights monitoring body.

According to Articles 21, 40 and 41 of the ICCPR alongside the Optional Protocol, the HRC performs four mechanisms of implementation. These mechanisms are: the examination of State reports, the adoption of general comments, the examination of individual communications as provided in the Optional Protocol and the consideration of interstate complaints. This study will mainly focus on the general comment function, since it is the most significant one of the four in terms of critically assessing the right to democracy. This analysis will also assess the State-reporting mechanism, since the focus will shift later on to State compliance with Article 25.

18 Article 28(2) of the ICCPR.
19 Article 28(1) of the ICCPR.
20 Article 32(1) of the ICCPR.
21 Ibid.
22 McGoldrick (n 4) 53.
23 Ibid.
24 Ibid.

'General Comments' have been described by some as a vague and misleading term.[25] It is indeed misleading in terms of the directed audience to receive such comments, however, the function is a very useful tool that benefits all State parties equally in various issues.[26] According to Steiner's commentary on the evolution of general comments,[27] the function has developed gradually in recent years in four phases: the first from 1981 to 1983; the second from 1984 to 1988; the third from 1989 to 1999 and the fourth which started in 2000. In the first phase, the HRC seemed to be rather hesitant and not confident in giving useful general comments.[28] The reason behind this is that the function was new to States, and there is a necessity for the HRC to act with caution in order to avoid confrontation with State representatives over procedural issues.[29] The second phase witnessed more detail and legal debate, however with political constraints. This is no surprise, since this phase was in the time of the Cold War. The third phase on the other hand came in the time when the Soviet sphere was declining, and was free from previous political restraints. This phase witnessed many useful general comments, especially those focusing on the issues of political participation and free and fair elections.[30] Finally, the fourth phase witnessed umbrella comments that consolidated the whole system with expansive and detailed examination.[31]

Nevertheless, the ICCPR came with an effective monitoring mechanism through the HRC that indeed helped to a very high extent in the development of our understanding in civil and political rights. In examining the general comments of the Committee, in addition to the large volume of case law, gives us an in-depth understanding of any right in question. This is not available when examining a declaration or any other soft-law instrument.

Further, the State-reporting mechanism is of vital importance, and is the only obligatory monitoring function under the Covenant.[32] The mechanism

25 P Alston, 'The Historical Origins of the Concept of 'General Comments' in Human Rights Law' in LB de Chazournes and VG Debbas (eds), *The International Legal System in Quest of Equity and Universality: Liber Amicorum, Georges Abi-Saab* (Kluwer Law International 2001) 763.

26 Ghandi (n 1) 25.

27 Steiner (n 4) 877–8.

28 This is clear in General Comments Nos 2 and 3.

29 The first three General Comments (which together constitute the first phase) were focused on procedural issues.

30 See General Comment 25.

31 For detailed illustrations of the four phases, see Steiner (n 4) 878–84.

32 S Joseph, J Schultz and M Castan, *The International Covenant on Civil and Political Rights: Cases, Material, and Commentary* (Oxford University Press 2000) 11. See also I Boerefijin, 'Towards a Strong System of Supervision: The Human Rights Committee's

was influenced by the longstanding practice of the International Labour Organisation.[33] All State parties are required under Article 40 to submit an initial report within a year of entry into force. The HRC required States to submit periodic reports once every five years.[34] The periodic reporting procedure was not explicitly mentioned in the Covenant, and was a product of the HRC, in order to establish a spirit of commitment, which was not uncommon in corresponding international human rights instruments.[35] The Committee may also request emergency reports in extraordinary circumstances.[36] The drafting history of the monitoring provision reveals a great deal of contention. The Soviet Bloc considered such procedure as a violation of sovereignty.[37] This indeed was a result of ideological orientation, where socialist nations favoured the focus on the economic, social and cultural aspects more than civil and political rights.

The HRC when examining a State report could rely on other sources of information. NGOs and human rights defenders could provide the Committee with parallel reports and additional information. Some States challenged the validity of such outreach by the HRC, on the basis that there was no legal authorization.[38] The HRC issues concluding observations on a State's report, highlighting the positive and negative aspects of the implementation of the Covenant, and its observations are usually accompanied by recommendations.[39]

However, what is concerning is that the HRC could be subject to political considerations. Although, as we have seen, its work has developed to a very high extent in the past years, the way in which its members are chosen and are eligible for re-election is highly questionable. Therefore, in order for it to have more credibility, it would have been better if the members were elected for a single non-renewable term only.

Moreover, the ICCPR came in an age when international law was the product of the sovereign will of States.[40] The Westphalian understanding of

---

Role in Reforming the Reports Procedure under Article 40 of the Covenant on Civil and Political Rights' (1995) 17 *HRQ* 766.

33 Nowak (n 4) 713.

34 UN Doc CCPR/C/19Rev. 1 (26 August 1982) para. 2.

35 For example, CEDAW, CERD, CAT and CRC all have similar procedures.

36 Joseph (n 32) 11; S Joseph, 'New Procedures Concerning the Human Rights Committee's Examination of State Reports' (1995) 13 *Netherlands Quarterly of Human Rights* 5, 15–23.

37 Nowak (n 4) 714.

38 McGoldbrick (n 4) 77–8.

39 Joseph (n 32) 12.

40 The *Lotus* Principle provided that international law 'governs rules between independent States. The rules of law binding upon States therefore emanate from their own free will'. *S S Lotus*, 1927 PCIJ Series A, No. 10.

international law dominated the international community at the time. However, international law has developed greatly in recent years. NGOs have a great role in promoting human rights and other important topics as well; in fact, some are considered by many as international legislators to a certain extent.[41] Therefore, with this rapidly developing status of global governance, accompanied with the developing 'binding' role of NGOs, the HRC needs to have a more positive role in addressing issues, or it will develop to be an irrelevant body in the foreseeable future.

Therefore, the HRC needs to have a greater role in addressing the issues raised in front of it given that international law has developed rapidly in recent years, especially in the sense that it gives a greater role to NGOs and its direct engagement with individuals, unlike what it was in the beginning of the last century. An effective monitoring mechanism will provide significant jurisprudence, necessary to interpret abstract terms for the favour of individuals whose fundamental rights to freedoms need to be protected, not limited to the right to democracy.

2.4 Article 25: the right to political participation

The right to political participation is the foundation of a democratic society. It is impossible to imagine a democratic society that cannot choose its representatives through genuine periodic elections, regardless of the form of democracy that society applies. However, the right to democracy cannot be limited to such procedure.

The right to free and fair elections encompasses both the right to stand (to be elected) and the right to vote. Article 21 of the UDHR provided that the will of the people is to be 'expressed in periodic and genuine elections', which is the first firm emphasis on the right with a universal status. However, as explained earlier, the corresponding provision in the UDHR provided a minimalist view that does not contribute significantly in the development of an international law of democracy. Therefore, it is of significance to assess the procedural understanding of the term in the context of Article 25 of the Covenant, in order to comprehend the scope of the procedural nature in its setting.

This part will assess the right to free and fair elections through basically evaluating Article 25 of the ICCPR in the light of the relevant General

41 See generally D Zaring, 'International Law by Other Means: The Twilight Existence of International Financial Regulatory Organizations' (1998) 33 *Texas International Law Journal* 281, 327; BZ Tamanaha, 'Understanding Legal Pluralism: Past to Present, Local to Global' (2007) 29 *Sydney Law Review* 19.

Comment and individual communications provided by the HRC, given that the ICCPR was the most involved universal document when it comes to the right in question, and will be the ideal instrument to critically assess with regard to the right. The focus will be on the limitation of the right to citizens, in contrast to other fundamental rights and freedoms, which are given to every individual on a universal basis. The concentration will be then shifted to the rights to vote and to be elected with reference to the relevant jurisprudence of the HRC in that respect. This section will provide a full illustration on how the rights involved provide a thin and limited understanding of a right to democracy, restricting it to the conduct of a number of electoral procedures on a periodic basis.

Article 25 of the Covenant provides:

> Every citizen shall have the right and the opportunity, without any of the distinctions mentioned in article 2 and without unreasonable restrictions:
>
> (a) To take part in the conduct of public affairs, directly or through freely chosen representatives;
> (b) To vote and to be elected at genuine periodic elections which shall be by universal and equal suffrage and shall be held by secret ballot, guaranteeing the free expression of the will of the electors;
> (c) To have access, on general terms of equality, to public service in his country.

Although the text did not explicitly refer to the term *democracy* and limited its terminology to the abstract notion of the right to political participation, the HRC clearly endorsed a minimalist view to the right to democracy. The Committee expressed in General Comment 25:

> Whatever form of constitution or government is in force, the Covenant requires States to adopt such legislative and other measures as may be necessary to ensure that citizens have an effective opportunity to enjoy the rights it protects.

Therefore, this does not only show a commitment to a marginal assurance to democratic governance, but a contradiction even in the protection of the procedural right to political participation, where the language is not firm to impose a positive obligation on States to adopt a democratic form of government.

The practice of the HRC continues in the jurisprudence that will be assessed in this section, where it limits the right to democracy to its procedural elements in the form of the conduct of free and fair elections on a periodic basis. This shows that, to the Committee, the right to democracy is *initially* the procedure of elections. This previous statement will be the cornerstone of the evaluation of Article 25 if the ICCPR.

The article generally focuses on three aspects: the right to take part in the conduct of public affairs; the right to vote and to be elected; and the right of equal access to public services – in addition to its limitation to citizens. These aspects will be discussed thoroughly.

a A right of citizens

The right to political participation is a right of citizens. Unlike other rights covered in the ICCPR, one can observe that the right to vote and to be elected has a rather different nature. All of the rights have a universal character except this one, which is restricted to citizens.[42] This restriction comes after an age when property owning was the only criteria for the right to vote in many countries.[43] This allowed aliens to vote where nations did not comprehend the notion of citizenship very well; instead, they referred to them as 'inhabitants'.[44] However, citizenship nevertheless connotes a commitment by the individual to the State and, thus, it is the best practical evidence of one's effective membership of a society.[45] Therefore, denying aliens the right to vote is considered justifiable to a very high extent.

A question arises as to the nature of such citizenship that qualifies one to practise the rights covered in Article 25. The HRC was clear that discrimination between citizens on the basis of birth or naturalization could foster issues of conformity with Article 25.[46] However, with reference to the general rule of reasonableness, a State could make some regulations on the practising of naturalized citizens of their right to political participation, as long as it is deemed reasonable and without discrimination on the basis of race, colour, language or ethnicity.

42 Another exception would be Article 13 of the ICCPR that applies to aliens only. A Conte, 'Democratic and Civil Rights' in A Conte and R Burchill (eds), *Defining Civil and Political Rights: The Jurisprudence of the United Nations Human Rights Committee* (2nd edn, Ashgate 2009) 97.

43 In the nineteenth century, many countries restricted the right to vote to property owners only. See generally K Porter, *A History of Suffrage in the United States* (Chicago University Press 1918).

44 GM Rosberg, 'Aliens and Equal Protection: Why Not the Right to Vote?' (1976) 75 *Michigan Law Review* 1093, 1096.

45 H Lardy, 'Citizenship and the Right to Vote' (1997) 17 *Oxford Journal of Legal Studies* 91, 92.

46 General Comment 25, para. 3.

Furthermore, citizens – whether by birth or naturalized – have not only the right, but also the opportunity to exercise political rights. By opportunity, a State should provide the measures necessary to ensure that citizens could exercise their right effectively. This is achieved through overcoming barriers and difficulties such as illiteracy, poverty, and obstacles associated with language and freedom of movement.[47]

The specific use of the term *citizen* in Article 25 came in order to avoid the ambiguity of the corresponding provision of the UDHR that gave the right to *everyone*. This specific limitation to citizens is more accurate and correct since, effectively, under the UDHR, State parties emphasized that it was a citizen's right. Therefore, the wording in the Covenant is nonetheless much more accurate than the Declaration in this respect. Therefore, it is important to acknowledge here that the citizen is the core element or unit a democratic society is built upon. This extends whether the right to democracy was defined in its procedural or substantive comprehension.

b The right to vote

The right to vote is one of the most important features of any democratic system. Paragraph (b) of Article 25 provided the right to vote and to be elected. Both rights go hand in hand since the representation system requires both elements. The Covenant provided that elections are to be periodic and genuine. Periodic elections means that they are to be held on a regular basis at the discretion of States, usually once every four to six years.[48] Genuine elections on the other hand mean that voters have certain influence on the turnout of the elections, through practising their right to vote amongst a number of political alternatives.[49] Therefore, with these guarantees, puppet elections cannot be used by States in order to fulfill the requirements of Article 25.

Voters practise their right in conformity with a number of internationally recognized voting principles. These principles include universal and equal suffrage, secret ballot and free elections. Universal suffrage means that the right to vote is permitted to all individuals and is not restricted to a certain class or group of people.[50] However, absolute universal suffrage through giving the right to vote to all members of society is deemed to be impractical and hard to achieve. Therefore, almost all nations restrict the right to

47 General Comment 25, paras 11, 12.
48 Nowak (n 4) 573.
49 Ibid.
50 Ibid 574.

vote to those that acquire legal capacity. This capacity excludes for instance minors, aliens and convicted criminals without constituting a violation to the principle.[51]

However, is excluding individuals on the basis of gender deemed a violation to the principle of universal suffrage and consequently the Covenant? The State of Kuwait issued a reservation on paragraph (b) to exclude women and members of the armed forces and police from the right to vote.[52] Although Kuwait was allowed to complete its accession to the Covenant, this reservation seems rather concerning.

The principle of equal suffrage on the other hand is less complicated to comprehend. It may be defined simply as: one person, one vote. The HRC stressed this principle in General Comment 25:

> The principle of one person, one vote, must apply, and within the framework of each State's electoral system, the vote of one elector should be equal to the vote of another. The drawing of electoral boundaries and the method of allocating votes should not distort the distribution of voters or discriminate against any group and should not exclude or restrict unreasonably the right of citizens to choose their representatives freely.[53]

This principle is very important in a democratic society, since it provides equality amongst all voters, regardless of their social status or personal wealth. The principle is applied not only through giving each voter the same voting weight as the other, but also it applies to the proportionate distribution of electoral districts. In *Matyus v Slovakia,* the HRC applied the principle of equal suffrage, when it found that it was violated in the way a number of municipal electoral districts were distributed out of proportionality which constituted a violation to *inter alia* Article 25(b) of the Covenant.[54] Therefore, States need to put proportionate distribution of electoral districts amongst their priorities.[55]

51 Ibid.

52 The State of Kuwait declared with regard to Article 25(b) of the ICCPR that 'The Government of Kuwait wishes to formulate a reservation with regard to article 25(b). The provisions of this paragraph conflict with the Kuwaiti electoral law, which restricts the right to stand and vote in elections to males. It further declares that the provisions of the article shall not apply to members of the armed forces or the police.' See United Nations, *Treaty Series*, vol. 999, 171.

53 General Comment 25, para. 21.

54 *Matyus v Slovakia*, Communication No. 923/2000, 22 July 2002. CCPR/C/75/D/923/2000. For more on the proportionality rationale see C Bell, 'Power Sharing and Human Rights Law' (2013) 17 *The International Journal of Human Rights* 204.

55 For more about equal suffrage, see RA Dahl and CE Lindblom, *Politics, Economics and Welfare* (Harper & Bros 1953); JW Still, 'Political Equality and Electoral Systems' (1984) 91 *Ethics* 375.

Furthermore, in order to guarantee free elections, voters must have the option not to vote. Compulsory voting systems do not guarantee free elections, since the voter is in a sense coerced into voting, facing a penalty for not doing so. Australia is the best example of a country that still applies a compulsory voting system. It applies the idea that voting is a civic duty rather than a political right.[56] However, in the view of this thesis, voting is a right not a duty, and members of society that choose to boycott an election should not be coerced into doing otherwise.[57] Moreover, the compulsory system cannot ensure 'an inelegant vote' which is based on certain political or national considerations, since people generally vote to avoid punishment, rather than willingly participating in the democratic process.[58]

The final voting principle is that of secret ballot.[59] Under secret ballot elections, voters cast their votes in secret, which is an important guarantee in the establishment of free elections. Under the secret ballot principle, minorities and opposition groups are protected and are able to cast their votes freely.[60] The secret ballot principle could be restricted in narrow circumstances, such as to allow the disabled and elderly to vote via the proxy of another individual.[61] However, no wider deviation from the principle is possible.

Today, most individuals are computer literate and have access to the Internet. This leads one to question the possibility of electronic elections. In addressing this question, one must first ask whether or not such elections are compatible with the ICCPR. The HRC has failed to address the issue in its General Comments; however, this has not stopped States from modernizing their electoral methods. Estonia, for instance, started applying this new system with its 2005 municipal election.[62] It was the first nation in the world to hold a binding Internet election. The government provided the general public with access to the databases and software related to the

56 See generally L Hill, 'Public Acceptance of Compulsory Voting: Explaining the Australian Case' (2010) 46 *Representation* 425, 438; I McAllister, 'Compulsory Voting, Turnout and Party Advantage in Australia' (1986) 21 *Australian Journal of Political Science* 89, 93.

57 Compulsory voting today is practiced in a small number of States including Australia.

58 CA Hughes, 'Compulsory Voting' (1966) 1 *Australian Journal of Political Science* 83.

59 The secret ballot principle was first introduced in modern times in Britain and France in the Eighteenth and Nineteenth Centuries. For more on its historical development see M Crook and T Crook, 'The Advent of the Secret Ballot in Britain and France, 1789–1914: From Public Assembly to Private Compartment' (2007) 92 *History* 449.

60 Nowak (n 4) 582.

61 Ibid 583.

62 See W Drechsler, 'Dispatch from the Future' *Washington Post* (5 November 2006).

election in order to be verified and audited, as a guarantee of the freedom of the election.[63] Furthermore, this new electoral method does not violate the principle of secret ballot; instead, it may be considered as a further guarantee of the secrecy of the vote.[64] However, the idea is nevertheless new and was not researched nor addressed by the HRC. Therefore, in order for the international community to have confidence in the new Internet-based election idea, the HRC needs to address the issue in detail to set out guidelines and boundaries that regulate the matter.

Moreover, paragraph (c) of Article 25 provided that citizens are to enjoy equal access to public services. This means that all administrative posts under the three branches of government are to be available to all citizens without discrimination in accordance with Article 2 of the ICCPR. In order to satisfy the requirements of the said paragraph, State parties are to provide objective and transparent measures for the appointment and promotion processes.[65] This includes such measures required for dismissal as well.[66] Therefore, it is important for the HRC to put firm guidelines in place in order to avoid any conflict in this respect.

In assessing the right to vote under the scope of the ICCPR, one may observe that it is an elaborate description of one of the main pillars of the procedural aspect of democracy. However, the vague wording provided in Article 25 of the Covenant makes it difficult to conclude that the right has been firmly established at the international level. The terms 'reasonable restrictions', 'public affairs', 'general terms of equality' and others are indeed vague and misleading. The reason behind this according to Nowak is that political rights (ie democracy) stand in the middle between civil rights on one hand and economic and social rights on the other and, therefore, it is very difficult to find a consensus between States in terms of definitions.[67] Therefore, it is important for the HRC to provide clear definitions in a general comment. This would represent a very significant contribution to enhancing the position of the procedural right to democracy in international law.

63 S Meagher, 'When Personal Computers Are Transformed into Ballot Boxes: How Internet Elections in Estonia Comply with the United Nations International Covenant on Civil and Political Rights' (2007) 23 *American University International Law Review* 365, 376.

64 Ibid 367.

65 Nowak (n 4) 585.

66 Ibid.

67 Ibid 590.

c The right to stand

Paragraph (a) of Article 25 provides a general right to take part in the conduct of public affairs. This allows the people of every nation to have a positive role in various aspects of their public interests. There is no specific model of democracy required by the ICCPR to apply this right; however, according to Nowak, if one imagined that this right is to be applied in a country with a parliamentary system, which is basically based on the principle of the separation of powers, the right will be limited to the election of the legislative authority.[68] This right is not violated if the head of State was not elected, or was in the form of a hereditary monarch, and judicial and executive positions were appointed directly by him/her, given that there is an elected legislator and the nation has a parliamentary model of democracy.[69] It is however violated if the head of State has wide autonomous influence and was not elected directly or indirectly by his people, which is the case in constitutional systems which do not separate the powers and are generally found in presidential republics and absolute monarchies.[70]

As to political parties, the HRC stressed that: 'The right of persons to stand for election should not be limited unreasonably by requiring candidates to be members of parties or of specific parties.'[71] It furthermore asserted that: 'Party membership should not be a condition of eligibility to vote, nor a ground of disqualification.'[72] In *Bwalya v Zambia*, the HRC addressed the issue of the one-party system and its compatibility with Covenant.[73] With regard to its violation of Article 25, the Committee concluded that:

> [The] author, a leading figure of a political party in opposition to the former President, has been prevented from participating in a general election campaign as well as from preparing his candidacy for this party. This amounts to an unreasonable restriction on the author's right to "take part in the conduct of public affairs" which the State party has failed to explain or justify. In particular, it has failed to explain the requisite conditions for participation in the elections. Accordingly, it must be assumed that Mr Bwalya was detained and denied the right to run for a parliamentary seat in the Constituency of Chifubu merely on

68 Ibid 570–1.
69 Ibid 571.
70 Ibid.
71 General Comment 25, para 17.
72 Ibid para. 10.
73 *Bwalya v Zambia,* Communication No. 314/1988, 27 July 1993. CCPR/C/48/D/314/1988.

> account of his membership in a political party other than that officially recognized; in this context, the Committee observes that restrictions on political activity outside the only recognized political party amount to an unreasonable restriction of the right to participate in the conduct of public affairs.[74]

However, the Committee seems to be rather hesitant in fully addressing the issue of a one-party system. This system should not be considered today as a democratic one, and the HRC should take a firm stand on the issue, regardless of any political considerations.

Moreover, on examining the individual communications associated with the right to stand in Article 25, one can find *Matyus v Slovakia* quite alarming.[75] The HRC found a violation of the principle of equal suffrage in terms of proportional distribution of voters in a number of electoral districts. However, its conclusion was based on that of the Constitutional Court of Slovakia. The Committee provided:

> As regards the question whether article 25 of the Covenant was violated, the Committee notes that the Constitutional Court of the State party held that by drawing election districts for the same municipal council with substantial differences between the number of inhabitants per elected representative, despite the election law which required those voting districts to be proportional to the number of inhabitants, the equality of election rights required by the State party's constitution was violated. In the light of this pronouncement, based on a constitutional clause similar to the requirement of equality in article 25 of the Covenant, and in the absence of any reference by the State party to factors that might explain the differences in the number of inhabitants or registered voters per elected representative in different parts of Rozòava, the Committee is of the opinion that the State party violated the author's rights under article 25 of the Covenant.[76]

Therefore, a legitimate question arises whether or not the Committee's conclusion would have been the same if the Constitutional Court had a different point of view or no view at all.[77] The answer to this may be found by examining another individual communication.

74 Ibid para. 6.6.
75 *Matyus v Slovakia* (n 54).
76 Ibid para. 9.2.
77 Nowak (n 4) 591.

In the very recent communication, *Paksas v Lithuania*, the Committee took a very significant step in not adhering to domestic legal systems.[78] The author, who served as president of Lithuania, had been given by his nation's constitutional court a lifelong prohibition against standing for presidential or parliamentary elections, and against holding the offices of prime minister, minister or judge on the grounds that he unconstitutionally provided a Russian businessman with Lithuanian citizenship. The HRC found such a lifelong constraint on the exercise of the right to stand for election an unreasonable restriction that violated the author's right under Article 25(b) and (c).[79]

However, HRC member Mr Gerald L. Neuman, provided in an individual dissenting comment that such lifelong prohibition was not a violation of the corresponding article, but also an extraordinary and necessary measure 'for protecting the democratic political process against an otherwise irremovable President who abuses the powers of the office'.[80] This observation is indeed a very valid one, especially when considering the protection of democracy against intolerant rhetoric, beyond the classic procedural limitations provided by international benchmarks including but not limited to the ICCPR.

Further, the right to vote and to be elected requires the application of the principle of free elections. This principle does not apply during the voting process only, but is also applied through a number of factors that must be accompanied with a democratic society. These factors must guarantee the voters freedom to choose their representatives through guaranteeing that equal opportunities are offered to all candidates in accordance with Article 25(a) as explained earlier.

Nowak asserts that the most significant guarantee of free elections is the application of a multi-party system.[81] Under this system, the voter is offered a number of alternatives for which he has the option to vote to. However, as mentioned earlier, the HRC still considers the one-party system to be a form of democratic government, which is nevertheless an obstacle in firmly establishing the principle of free elections at the international level.[82]

In *Korneenko v Belarus* the HRC linked Article 25 with the freedom of expression as provided in Article 19 of the Covenant.[83] The author, whilst

78 *Paksas v Lithuania*, Communication No. 2155/2012, 21 March 2014. CCPR/C/110/D/2155/2012.
79 Ibid para. 9.
80 Ibid, Appendix.
81 Nowak (n 4) 584.
82 Ibid.
83 *Korneenko v Belarus*, Communication No. 1226/2003, 20 July 2012. CCPR/C/105/D/1226/2003.

campaigning for the opposition presidential candidate, was stopped by traffic police who confiscated campaign material (leaflets) from his vehicle. The relevant administrative court ruled that the seizure was lawful under Belarusian law. The HRC considered the act as a violation of Article 25, on the grounds that the free communication of ideas – as provided in electoral material – was necessary for the conduct of free and fair election.[84]

Similarly, in *Jong-Cheol v Republic of Korea*, the Committee found that the Korean Election Act violated Articles 19 and 25(a) and (b) on the basis that the ban on the publication of election polls amounted to a violation of the Covenant.[85] Therefore, it is safe to say the HRC complemented the doctrinal text of the Covenant with interpretive jurisprudence. From this one can conclude that the particulars addressed in the aforementioned communications are necessary to fully comprehend the right to political participation in its procedural context.

Further, in addition to citizenship, knowledge of a language may also be deemed as a reasonable restriction on the right to stand and should not violate the principle of universal suffrage in that context. In *Ignatane v Latvia,* the HRC considered the language restrictions of the Latvian government on the right to stand for public office unreasonable and discriminatory.[86] The Committee provided:

> The Committee concludes that Mrs. Ignatane has suffered specific injury in being prevented from standing for the local elections in the city of Riga in 1997, because of having been struck off the list of candidates on the basis of insufficient proficiency in the official language. The Human Rights Committee considers that the author is a victim of a violation of article 25, in conjunction with article 2 of the Covenant.[87]

84 Ibid para. 8.4.

85 *Jong-Cheol v Republic of Korea*, Communication No. 968/2001, 27 July 2005. CCPR/C/84/D/968/2001, para. 8.3, 9. For more on similar observations where the HRC concluded on violations of Article 25 of the Covenant, see *Diergaardt et al. v Namibia*, Communication No. 760/1997, 25 July 2000. CCPR/C/69/D/760/1997; *Paraga v Croatia*, Communication No. 727/1996, 4 April 2001. CCPR/C/71/D/727/1996; *Mazou v Cameroon*, Communication No. 630/1995, 3 August 2001. CCPR/C/72/D/630/1995; *Dissanayake. Sri Lanka*, Communication No. 1373/2005, 22 July 2005. CCPR/C/93/D/1373/2005; *Bandaranayake v Sri Lanka*, Communication No. 1376/2007, 24 July 2008. CCPR/C/93/D/1376/2005.

86 *Ignatane v Latvia*, Communication No. 884/1999, 31 July 2001. CCPR/C/72/D/884/1999.

87 Ibid para. 7.5.

Yet, where such restrictions were not intended to exclude linguistic minorities there is no valid reason to consider them incompatible with the principle of universal suffrage.

In *Debreczeny v Netherlands*, the Committee concluded on another reasonable restriction on the right to be elected.[88] This was based on the standard of conflict of interest, where the author who was a civil servant (police sergeant) was denied to submit his credentials after winning a local election, on the basis that both of his capacities were under the administration of the same local official and conflicting in the nature.[89]

From the previous jurisprudence of the HRC, in terms of its consideration of State reports, individual communications and General Comment 25; one can safely assert that the right to democracy in the context of the ICCPR is a procedural one. The jurisprudence provided an extended framework on the scope and context of such right, in terms of its limitation to citizens, its encompassment of the rights to vote and to be elected within certain reasonable measures. However, it failed to address some necessary issues regarding definitions and restrictions in necessary detail. Nonetheless, it is important to comprehend, that such a minimalist procedural view of the right in question cannot be sufficient to be a significant part in the development of the right to democracy in international law.

In short, the right to free and fair elections under the ICCPR is not strong enough under the current wording of Article 25. It is furthermore weakened by the performance of the HRC, through its positive presentation with regard to its response to individual communications regarding the said Article, and, its negative performance through not providing clear definitions in a general comment to the vague wording of Article 25. This is of course due partially to political considerations and ideological polarization. However, properly establishing a right of political participation in international law needs to focus on the substantive element of the entitlement, beyond limiting it to the procedure of periodic free and fair elections.

88 *Debreczeny v Netherlands*, Communication No. 500/1992, 3 April 1995. CCPR/C/53/D/500/1992.

89 Ibid para. 9.3. For more HRC conclusions on non-violation of Article 25 of the Covenant and examples of reasonable restrictions, see *Gillot v France*, Communication No. 932/2000, 26 July 2002. CCPR/C/75/D/932/2000; *Jacobs v Belgium*, Communication No. 943/2000, 17 August 2004. CCPR/C/81/D/943/2000.

2.5 Conclusion

This chapter has discussed in detail the procedural right to democracy in the context of the ICCPR. It presented that the content and scope of such understanding of the right in question is limited to the procedure of periodic free and fair elections, which is a significant conceptual problem. This thin electoral model cannot be applied in transitional societies, where a democratic tradition is not robustly found and could therefore lead to the failure of the sustainability of democratic governance through its theoretical and practical admission of intolerant actors in the system.

The chapter also presented that significant international instrument provided that the right to democracy was limited to citizens, with a simple illustration of the scope of the procedures prescribed in the conduct of periodic elections. Such limitation to citizens is necessary and reasonable; however, the wording and commentary on Articles 25 of the ICCPR is nonetheless inconclusive. The failure to have reference to clear and unambiguous terms makes it difficult to determine State practice and a rational reflection on where the position of the right to democracy in this context stands in international law.

Further, there is no question that the right to democracy in the context of the UDHR and ICCPR was subject to political polarization in the Cold War era. This nevertheless influenced the limitation of the right to procedural terms. Therefore, it is important to extend the evaluation to wider developments in international law, to include the expansions in the understanding of the right to democracy in the period that followed the collapse of the Soviet Union.

The right to democracy in international law developed beyond this minimalist view to incorporate other rights and fundamental freedoms, which are mutually reinforcing. Hence, the limitations provided in the context of the procedural understanding provide a very basic minimalist view that can only be seen as an element in the right to democracy in international law, but not the whole picture. Therefore, the discussion must extend to assess the substantive element of the right to democracy through evaluating other sources of international law that have developed beyond ideological considerations and conceptual limitations.

3 The substantive right to democracy in international law

3.1 Introduction

The previous chapters provided a detailed assessment of the right to democracy in international law, as stipulated in the context of Articles 21 and 25 of the UDHR and ICCPR. These instruments understood democracy as a series of procedures in the form of the right of citizens to vote and be elected in periodic free and fair elections. Such limitation reflects a minimalist view that cannot contribute significantly in the development of a right to democracy in international law. This procedural conceptualization is therefore a significant conceptual problem that cannot answer the main questions associated with the escalation of political intolerance in transitional societies, especially in the context of recent events in the Arab World which led to a dramatic rise of intolerant political Islamist actors, through the means of free and fair elections.

This chapter will provide with detail the wider developments in international law, which led to the creation of a substantive view of democracy. This substantive conceptualization could be defined according to Gregory Fox as 'a series of rights that are collectively reinforcing'.[1] Therefore, it extends way beyond the limitation to free and fair elections on a periodic basis. The substantive account incorporates a number of other rights that are necessary for the sustainability of democracy, and not to be used as a means to reach power in order to abolish the democratic system. It does in other words provide conceptual and legal guarantees for the protection of democracy.

1 GH Fox, 'Democracy, Right to, International Protection' in R Wolfrum (ed.), *Max Planck Encyclopedia of Public International Law* (Oxford University Press 2013) para. 10.

The substantive account of democracy enforces the notion that democracy is more than a means to reach power. It is an end in itself and a necessity for the free advancement of the fundamental capabilities of all members of society.[2] Democracy is also 'about debate and solving differences through non-violent means'.[3] This full understanding of the notion of democracy can only be achieved through the application of a comprehensive legal model, which stretches beyond the procedural aspect to incorporate a series of fundamental rights and freedoms that are reciprocally reinforcing.

After the collapse of the Soviet Union in the early 1990s, the international community took bolder steps in the enforcement of a right to democracy in international law.[4] International organizations had a significant role in redefining the right in question beyond its procedural element and the limitations imposed by Cold War ideological polarizations. The role of international organizations in this respect is significant, where they provided a shared platform for consideration of fundamental human rights issues.[5] However, it is important to keep in mind that there are 'limited carrots and sticks' available to such organizations while promoting an effective substantive account of democracy.[6] There is no question that international law in this regard is determined by State practice which international organizations cannot forcefully impose in many cases. But nonetheless, one cannot deny that the role of such organizations is effective in setting standards and changing conceptual understanding, especially in the context of the developing right to democracy in international law.

The importance of the consideration of the substantive account is not only significant in terms of determining the development of the right to democracy in international law, but also to comprehend the framework and limitations of tolerance in a democratic society. Gregory Fox addressed the issue of political intolerance and international law's reaction to it from a distinctive and practical perspective in a joint paper with Georg Nolte, 'Intolerant

2 CB Macpherson, *The Real World of Democracy* (Clarendon Press 1966) 37.

3 R Burchill, 'The Developing International Law of Democracy' (2001) 64 *The Modern Law Review* 123, 129.

4 A great deal of literature was dedicated to Thomas Franck's idea of a democratic entitlement, which emerged in the period that followed the collapse of the Soviet Union. However, this book rejects the idea of the entitlement, given that it links the right to democracy to self-determination. For more, see introduction of book.

5 R Burchill, 'Regional Integration and the Promotion and Protection of Democracy in Asia: Lessons from ASEAN' (2009) 13 *Asian Yearbook of International Law* 113, 123.

6 GH Fox and BR Roth (eds), *Democratic Governance and International Law* (Cambridge University Press 2000) 9.

Democracies'.[7] The article came to address the problem of political intolerance and to answer the question of how a democracy could protect itself against anti-democratic actors while still remaining democratic. For this purpose, Fox and Nolte presented Algeria as a case study, where the democratic system was threatened by a fundamentalist Islamist group, through its advancement in the nation's 'free and fair' democratic parliamentary election. The Algerian military did not accept the result of the election, in order to save the nation's republican status and democratic institutions.[8] This Algerian scenario was compared with Hitler's rise to power, through free and fair elections which led to the fall of the Weimar Republic in Germany, and the dreadful consequences that followed.[9]

To assess the situation of democracy's response to political intolerance, Fox and Nolte provided a procedural and substantive understanding of democratic tolerance. The procedural view is limited to periodic free and fair elections, where it regulates 'decision-making but does not prescribe the decisions themselves'.[10] This is indeed similar to the position of the Human Rights Committee in General Comment 25, which disregards the threat of political intolerance and the rise of totalitarianism through free and fair elections.

The substantive account on the other hand views democracy – free and fair elections – as not an end in itself, but as a means to enforce other individual rights and freedoms.[11] The right to democracy is not 'absolute' in the sense that it could eliminate itself or abolish other fundamental political and civil freedoms.[12] This comparison and assessment of the precise aspect of political intolerance makes one important assumption, which is that the procedural understanding of the right to democracy makes the right toothless against anti-democratic actors. In other words, the right to periodic free and fair elections does not necessarily mean a right to democracy.[13]

The main point of the previous examples is that the application of the minimalist procedural understanding of democracy is not enough to guarantee

7 GH Fox and G Nolte, 'Intolerant Democracies' (1995) 36 *Harvard International Law Journal* 1.

8 Ibid 6–9.

9 Ibid 10–11.

10 Ibid 14.

11 Ibid 16.

12 Ibid.

13 For a response to *Intolerant Democracies*, see M Koskenniemi, 'Intolerant Democracies: A Reaction' (1996) 37 *Harvard International Law Journal* 231; BR Roth, 'Democratic Intolerance: Observations on Fox and Nolte' (1996) 37 *Harvard International Law Journal* 235.

the continuation of democratic governance. The necessity to look beyond the procedural limitations is of vital importance to comprehend the developing right to democracy in international law. For this purpose, this chapter will extend the assessment to include wider developments in international law in that respect.

This chapter will present the substantive right to democracy in international law as provided by international organizations and regional judicial decisions – in the context of the European Court of Human Rights (ECtHR) – which had a significant role in the definition and development of the notion. It will start by providing the role of international organizations in the redefinition of the procedural understanding of the right to democracy, which extends way beyond the traditional notion provided in the context of the UDHR and ICCPR, where it provided a more detailed and elaborated guarantee for free and fair elections. The assessment will then extend to include a number of Secretary-General's agendas that emphasized a new conceptualization of the term, beyond the Cold War limitations. This will be followed by an analysis of the content and scope of other rights collectively associated with the right to democracy in the context of the Vienna Declaration and Programme of Action and a selection of the Commission on Human Rights and UNGA resolutions related to substantive democracy. The evaluation will finally include an analysis of selected cases considered by the ECtHR on the right to democracy, and the reasonable limitations the Court addressed which extended the notion beyond its procedural setting. The chapter will conclude on where the substantive and procedural accounts of democracy stand in international law, especially in terms of the practice of States and international organizations.

3.2 Procedural shortcomings

The rights to vote and to be elected are important ingredients of the procedural aspect of political participation. The UDHR and ICCPR provided a very basic coverage of these rights. A number of necessary specifics in order to avoid State misconduct were not covered in both the original texts and relevant jurisprudence. In contrast, the Inter-Parliamentary Council's Declaration on the Criteria of Free and Fair Elections (DFFE) came with a lot of detail in addressing the issue.[14] The DFFE will be assessed in this section because it provides a number of mutually

14 Declaration on Criteria for Free and Fair Elections, adopted by the Inter-Parliamentary Council at its 154th Session, Paris, 26 March 1994.

reinforcing rights the application of the right to free and fair elections. With this respect, Article 2 provided:

> (1) Every adult citizen has the right to vote in elections, on a non-discriminatory basis.
> (2) Every adult citizen has the right to access to an effective, impartial and non-discriminatory procedure for the registration of voters.
> (3) No eligible citizen shall be denied the right to vote or disqualified from registration as a voter, otherwise than in accordance with objectively verifiable criteria prescribed by law, and provided that such measures are consistent with the State's obligations under international law.
> (4) Every individual who is denied the right to vote or to be registered as a voter shall be entitled to appeal to a jurisdiction competent to review such decisions and to correct errors promptly and effectively.
> (5) Every voter has the right to equal and effective access to a polling station in order to exercise his or her right to vote.
> (6) Every voter is entitled to exercise his or her right equally with others and to have his or her vote accorded equivalent weight to that of others.
> (7) The right to vote in secret is absolute and shall not be restricted in any manner whatsoever.

The language used here is very clear and straightforward unlike the vagueness of the ICCPR. It narrowed down the right to vote to *adult citizens* instead of *citizens* as the Covenant and other corresponding instruments provided. This shows that this Declaration is indeed a right step in the road to democratic enhancement on the international level.

Revisiting the right to vote is in the light of a number of factors, namely, voter registration, civic education and voter information, media access and the conduct of political parties. Voter registration may be considered as one of the most significant elements in assessing the success of a certain election.[15] Registering voters in an official electoral list is indeed the most important feature of a free and fair election. Through this measure, electoral fraud is minimalized if not totally abolished. However, a problem arises in updating the electoral list. This is because it requires a large scale of effort and funds that are very difficult to provide, especially in countries that suffer

15 G Goodwin-Gill, *Free and Fair Elections: International Law and Practice* (Inter-Parliamentary Union 1994) 131–2.

internal turmoil and instability. Nevertheless, the ideal way to provide such catalogues is through providing provisional lists that are published in local papers and other media outlets and are subject to objection. The registration process is assisted by political parties and candidates that examine the provisional lists to insure the registration of their supporters.[16]

Civic education is also of vital importance in terms of the right to vote, especially in developing countries. The voter's knowledge of the structure of the State, legislative body and his/her nation's constitution will indeed enhance the right to vote. It will develop even more if the voter had enough information about the voting process, time and location. The UNTAC provided a very useful and successful political education programme in Cambodia that lead to the improvement of the voting system in this developing Asian country that had a long history of electoral misconduct.[17] However, such education programme must be undertaken by local governments and national institutions. In Western democracies and developed States, civic education is taught in schools and is an essential part of the curriculum.[18] This needs to be implemented in developing countries gradually through democratic and political institutions, and then through higher and primary education.

Civic education needs to emphasize the issues of citizenship and Statehood. Through these two important topics, the voter will understand his duties and liabilities on an individual and collective basis. Only then could the voter perform his right to vote based on an educated choice.[19]

Media access is also of vital importance in the enforcement of the right to vote. When candidates are given equal access to the media, the general public could make an effective choice through choosing between a number of valid options. Voters could observe their candidates' manifestos and electoral programmes and discuss them through interactive debates. However, this requires that the media outlets be not monopolized by the State. If the State owned or controlled the media, the right to vote will not be practised properly. Therefore, in order for granting candidates equal access to the media, the State must allow the establishment of private media outlets with minimal governmental control and regulation.[20]

16 Ibid 133.

17 See generally, IPU, *Report of the IPU Election Observer Mission, Cambodia, 16 May–4 June 1993* as cited in Goodwin-Gill (n 15) 133.

18 Ibid 134.

19 See generally, H Brighouse, 'Civic Education and Liberal Legitimacy' (1998) 108 *Ethics* 719; WA Galston, 'Civic Education and Political Participation' (2004) 37 *Political Science and Politics* 263.

20 Goodwin-Gill (n 15) 150. See generally, M Prior, 'News vs. Entertainment: How Increasing Media Choice Widens Gaps in Political Knowledge and Turnout' (2005) 49 *American Journal of Political Science* 577.

Moreover, election management is also essential to the right to political participation. The electoral administration needs to be independent and accompanied by effective judicial remedies.[21] The establishment of an independent electoral commission, comprised of judges and other professional legal experts will establish a tradition of impartiality and professionalism. Eastern European countries established such commissions in their transitional process to democratic governance and it has proven to be effective.[22] However, giving the electoral management to a high judicial authority (ie constitutional court) will also be effective and impartial.

Electoral dispute settlement is also important to maintain the right to vote.[23] Although international benchmarks failed to address this issue directly, it is nevertheless of vital importance in the implementation of the right to vote. Many disputes may arise with regard to the interpretation of electoral laws, misconduct of the election administration and other disputes. Therefore, the need to provide an effective dispute settlement mechanism is necessary to ensure the integrity and impartiality of the election administration, and indeed to ensure that the right to vote is not violated.

The revisiting of the procedural aspects of the right to democracy, as echoed in the rights to vote and to be elected is of vital importance in order to realize the full characteristics of the entitlement. The vagueness of the rights involved in the ICCPR and other legal instruments makes the issue of application subject to ambiguous State discretion. Therefore, the consideration of the issues mentioned earlier in State practice would certainly enhance the incomplete procedural element of the right to democracy as it currently stands in significant international instruments. The aforementioned remedies to the classical procedural understanding of the right to democracy widen the minimalist view to incorporate a number of *procedural rights*. The adoption of the previous conceptualization is therefore necessary to extend the understanding to include the substantive account of the right to democracy in international law.

3.3 The role of international organizations

International organizations had a significant role in the redefinition of the right to democracy in international law beyond the minimalist procedural understanding. This was due to the collapse of the Soviet Bloc and the

21 Goodwin-Gill (n 15) 120.
22 Ibid 121.
23 Ibid 157.

democratization of many Eastern European nations, and the end of political stagnation, which led to a conceptual evolution.

The development of the conceptualization of the right to democracy in international law has advanced since the early 1990s. The UN Secretary-General issued a number of significant reports that emphasized the substantive right to democracy. The *Agenda for Peace* document underscored that democracy required 'respect for peace and fundamental freedoms'.[24] It also stressed that democracy was essential to 'attain peace', which is a significant statement in the development of the understanding of the right to democracy in international law.[25]

The Secretary-General issued another significant document dedicated to democracy, *Agenda for Democratization*.[26] This important report illustrated the role of the UN in the promotion of democracy in the international community through the introduction of a 'culture of democracy'.[27] The culture of democracy is a concept that is based on tolerance and non-violence and a societal consensus on peaceful transfer of power.[28] It stresses the fundamental pillars of democracy and a series of mutually reinforcing rights and freedoms necessary for the sustainability of democracy. The report provided:

> Democracy is not an affirmation of the individual at the expense of the community; it is through democracy that individual and collective rights, the rights of persons and the rights of peoples, can be reconciled. Many different balances can be struck between the rights of individuals and the rights of the community within the context of democratic politics. Democratic processes are the most reliable way to ensure that these balances are genuinely reflective of a people's broader culture, which, in every society, must itself serve as the ballast for the healthy functioning of democracy.[29]

The Secretary-General issued a subsequent report in 2005, *In Larger Freedom: Towards Development, Security and Human Rights for All*.[30] This

24 *An Agenda for Peace: Preventive Diplomacy, Peacemaking and Peacekeeping* (17 June 1992) UN Doc A/47/277 – S/24111, para. 81.

25 Ibid para. 82.

26 *An Agenda for Democratization* (20 December 1996) UN Doc A/51/761. For a detailed assessment on the drafting of this document, see CE Lombardo, 'The Making of an Agenda for Democratization: A Speechwriter's View' (2001) 2 *Chicago Journal of International Law* 253.

27 *An Agenda for Democratization* para. 24. See Burchill (n 5) 121.

28 Ibid para. 21.

29 Ibid para. 23.

30 *In Larger Freedom: Towards Development, Security and Human Rights for All* (21 March 2005) UN Doc A/59/2005.

report reaffirmed the commitment to the substantive right to democracy, and called for the establishment of a UN Democracy Fund to assist nations in establishing and strengthening their democratic institutions.[31]

Other international organizations and platforms contributed in the development of the right to democracy in international law. The Vienna Declaration and Programme of Action had a suggestive role in the definition of the term. The Declaration provided:

> Democracy, development and respect for human rights and fundamental freedoms are interdependent and mutually reinforcing. Democracy is based on the freely expressed will of the people to determine their own political, economic, social and cultural systems and their full participation in all aspects of their lives. In the context of the above, the promotion and protection of human rights and fundamental freedoms at the national and international levels should be universal and conducted without conditions attached. The international community should support the strengthening and promoting of democracy, development and respect for human rights and fundamental freedoms in the entire world.[32]

From the previous, one could safely observe that democracy is strongly linked with the protection of fundamental rights and freedoms. This extends beyond the minimalists' procedural view of the term, and takes it beyond the limitations of elitism and exclusiveness to make it a right to all of the people determined by their *genuine* will. This is significant where it links democracy to development and other fundamental outcomes, not limited to the understanding that it is a form of government with the intention to reach power.

The United Nations Commission on Human Rights Resolution *Promotion of the Right to Democracy* provided a list of the rights necessary to the full application of the right to democracy. This approach gave the right to democracy in international law a substantive dimension, which nevertheless contributes in its development. The Commission integrated the following rights to the right to democracy:

(a) the rights to freedom of opinion and expression, of thought, conscience and religion, and of peaceful association and assembly;

31 The UN Democracy Fund (UNDEF) was established in 2005, with the mandate to provide assistance and aid to transitional societies and developing democracies.

32 UNGA, *Vienna Declaration and Programme of Action* (12 July 1993) UN Doc A/CONF.157/23, para. 8.

(b) the right to freedom to seek, receive and impart information and ideas through any media;
(c) the rule of law, including legal protection of citizens' rights, interests and personal security, and fairness in the administration of justice and independence of the judiciary;
(d) the right of universal and equal suffrage, as well as free voting procedures and periodic and free elections;
(e) the right of political participation, including equal opportunity for all citizens to become candidates;
(f) transparent and accountable government institutions;
(g) the right of citizens to choose their governmental system through constitutional or other democratic means;
(h) the right to equal access to public services in one's own country.[33]

Therefore, democracy is seen in this view as a set of rights that are to be forced collectively. Applying this understanding is very useful to transitional democracies. The problem many developing nations face in their democratic transition is the view that the right to democracy is limited to the right to free and fair elections. The substantive view incorporates a series of measures that insure *inter alia* tolerance, pluralism and the rights of minorities.

The UN General Assembly also contributed to the extension of the right to democracy beyond its procedural understanding. In its *United Nations Millennium Declaration*, the General Assembly stressed that the 'will of the people' is the best assurance for the protection of fundamental rights and freedoms.[34] The General Assembly reaffirmed its commitment to the substantive right to democracy in the *2005 World Summit Outcome*, where it stated that the protection of human rights and democratic governance are 'interlinked' and 'mutually reinforcing'.[35]

The role of international organizations as delivered in the previous context provided a common ground for comprehending the right to democracy in international law. Limiting the observation of the right to international instruments that were adopted during the era of the Cold War and the ideological polarization associated with it is certainly not enough. The developing right to democracy in international law therefore cannot be limited to the minimalist procedural view. This substantive account as provided

33 UN Commission on Human Rights, *Promotion of the Right to Democracy* (27 April 1999) UN Doc E/CN.4/RES/1999/57, para. 2.
34 UNGA, *United Nations Millennium Declaration* (8 September 2000) UN Doc A/Res/55/2, para. 6.
35 UNGA, *2005 World Summit Outcome* (24 October 2005) UN Doc A/Res/60/1, para. 119.

by international organizations should thus be held in serious account when assessing the position of the right to democracy in international law, where it did – without the slightest doubt – contribute to its development. However, one cannot unquestionably assume that the aforementioned advances led to the development of international customary law on substantive democracy.[36]

3.4 The role of regional organizations and the European Court of Human Rights

Regional organizations also had a significant role in the definition and commitment to the right to democracy in international law. This is partly due to their un-attachment to the ideological polarization that surfaced during the Cold War era. The most significant organizations that reaffirmed commitment to democracy are the European Union (EU), the Organization of American States (OAC), the Commonwealth of Nations and the Organization of African Unity (AU).[37]

The Treaty on European Union (Maastricht Treaty) had a significant role in the determination of the political system in the EU.[38] It limited membership of the organization to democratic governments, as prescribed in the European Convention on Human Rights (ECHR).[39] Similarly, the OAS specified preconditions for membership in the Protocol of Washington, where it provided that members whose democratically elected government was removed by force may be suspended from the Organization's General Assembly.[40] The OAS also adopted Resolution 1080, which was intended to address the issue of military *coup d'états*.[41] Although it did not prescribe a course of action, the Resolution is significant in affirming the maintenance of democratic governance.[42]

The Secretary-General of the Commonwealth also expressed great concern when the elected leader of a member nation, Pakistan, was ousted

36 Burchill (n 3) 122.

37 Although the Commonwealth of Nations is not technically a regional organization, the author preferred to add it to this section for the conformity with the thematic approach of assessment.

38 European Union (EU), Treaty on European Union (Consolidated Version), Treaty of Maastricht, 7 February 1992, entry into force: 1 November 1993.

39 Article F.

40 Organization of American States (OAS), Protocol of Amendments to the Charter of the Organization of American States (Protocol of Washington), 14 December 1992, entry into force: 25 September 1997.

41 OAS Resolution 1080 (5 June 1991) AG/RES. 1080 (XXI-O/91).

42 Fox (n 1) para. 28.

from power by a *coup d'état* in 1999.[43] The Organization took some measures against the country through the appointment of an Action Group; and the nation's membership was eventually suspended. The Commonwealth suspended other nations following the interruption of democratic governance. This was the case in Nigeria, Zimbabwe and Fuji.[44] Likewise, the AU condemned military coups and reaffirmed democracy as the only form of government within its member States. It recently temporarily suspended the membership of Egypt after the army's coup against the nation's elected Islamist leader, invoking Article 30 of its Constitutive Act.[45] Egypt however had its membership restored after adhering to free and fair presidential elections.

From the previous, one could observe that the role of the aforementioned regional organizations had a decisive impact in affirming democracy as a form of government. Perhaps, the most compelling and elaborative of the previous examples is found in the European context, where it provided a significant point of reference to the ECHR, which has a great deal of jurisprudence that helped understand and define democracy, beyond its procedural context. From this, an assessment of the case law associated with the right to democracy is necessary to fully comprehend the nature and scope of the substantive right in this context.

The initial position of the ECtHR on democracy is that it is all about pluralism. The Court confirmed the substantive account of democracy in *Handyside v United Kingdom*.[46] The Court concluded:

> The Court's supervisory functions oblige it to pay the utmost attention to the principles characterising a 'democratic society'. Freedom of expression constitutes one of the essential foundations of such a society, one of the basic conditions for its progress and for the development of every man.[47]

Here, the ECtHR integrated the freedom of expression with democracy, which confirms its substantive understanding of the notion. The integration

43 See letter dated 20 October 1999 from the Permanent Representative of Canada to the UN addressed to the President of the Security Council UN Doc S/1999/1095.

44 Fox (n 1) para. 32.

45 Organization of African Unity (AU), Constitutive Act of the African Union, 1 July 2000, entry into force: 26 May 2001.

46 *Handyside v United Kingdom*, Series A No. 24 (1979/80).

47 Para. 49 of the judgment. A similar conclusion was reached in *Jersild v Denmark*, Series A No. 298 (1994) para. 37 of the judgment.

of such right to the understanding of a democratic society is significant, since it takes the whole notion of democracy beyond the restraints provided in the procedural understanding of the term, limiting democracy to the series of periodic elections. However, one cannot safely say from the jurisprudence of the Court that it provided a complete illustration of a democratic society, although it confirmed the pillars of pluralism, tolerance, freedom of expression, equality and liberty.[48]

In the case of the *United Communist Party of Turkey and Others v Turkey*, the ECtHR took a serious step in the protection of pluralism and tolerance as essential ingredients of democracy.[49] The Court concluded that the Turkish Constitutional Court's decision to dissolve the party on the grounds of its name, *Communist*, and its peaceful political campaign for Turkish and Kurdish separation as a violation of Article 11 of the ECHR.[50]

In contrast, the Court had a very different view in *Refah Partisi (Welfare Party) and Others v Turkey*.[51] The Refah Party came to power in Turkey, and was eventually dissolved by the Turkish judiciary on the grounds of its contradiction with the constitutional principles of secularism. The decision was appealed in Strasbourg, where the Court concurred with the decision to

48 JG Merrills, *The Development of International Law by the European Court of Human Rights* (Manchester University Press 1993) chapters 7 and 8; C Ovey and RCA White, *The European Convention on Human Rights* (4th edn, Oxford University Press 2006) 233.

49 *United Communist Party of Turkey and Others v Turkey* (App. 19392/92), Judgment of 30 January 1998 (1998) para. 45 of the judgment.

50 Article 11 of the ECHR states:

> 1 Everyone has the right to freedom of expression. This right shall include freedom to hold opinions and to receive and impart information and ideas without interference by public authority and regardless of frontiers. This article shall not prevent States from requiring the licensing of broadcasting, television or cinema enterprises.
>
> 2 The exercise of these freedoms, since it carries with it duties and responsibilities, may be subject to such formalities, conditions, restrictions or penalties as are prescribed by law and are necessary in a democratic society, in the interests of national security, territorial integrity or public safety, for the prevention of disorder or crime, for the protection of health or morals, for the protection of the reputation or rights of others, for preventing the disclosure of information received in confidence, or for maintaining the authority and impartiality of the judiciary.

The ECtHR also reaffirmed 'effective political democracy' with reference to Article 3 of Protocol 1 of the ECHR. See *Mathieu-Mohin and Clerfayt v Belgium*, Judgment of 2 March 1987, Series A, No. 113 (1988) para. 47 of the judgment; *Mathews v United Kingdom* (App. 24833/94), Judgment of 18 February 1999 (1999) para. 42 of the judgment.

51 *Refah Partisi (Welfare Party) and others v Turkey* (Apps. 41340/98, 41342/98 and 41344/98), Judgment of the Grand Chamber of 13 February 2003.

dissolve the party on the grounds of the incompatibility of its aims with the ECHR. The Court concluded:

> The Court considers that a political party may promote a change in the law or the legal and constitutional structures of the State on two conditions: firstly, the means used to that end must be legal and democratic; secondly, the change proposed must itself be compatible with fundamental democratic principles.[52]

The previous *Refah Principle* advanced by the ECtHR provides a significant contribution to the substantive account of democracy. It provides a democratic formula by which political actors who are intolerant to democracy could be excluded from the democratic process all together. The most significant aspect of this principle is that it implied that secularism was a fundamental element of democracy and provided a legal framework to justify limitations on tolerance in a democratic manner. The aim of such conformation of secularism and the limitation provided on tolerance is nonetheless the maximization of the application of democracy (widely and narrowly defined).

The Court's conclusion caused some controversy.[53] It failed to provide an in-depth evaluation of the political ideology of Refah. Understanding the ideological roots of the group is essential to realize its compatibility with democracy. Having its own conception of the good reflected in its distinctive and exclusive comprehensive doctrine could be very problematic to the issue of sustainable democratic governance.

However, one can assert that it is necessary for a democratic State to be tolerant of difference, but it must not be tolerant towards the intolerant that seeks the destruction of the democratic system.[54] Therefore, a restriction on such intolerant political activity needs to be considered as a reasonable limitation to the right to political participation based not necessarily solely on the principle of secularism.[55]

52 Para. 98 of the Judgment.

53 See K Boyle, 'Human Rights, Religion and Democracy: The Refah Partisi Case' (2004) 1 *Essex Human Rights Review* 1; TM Smith, 'Between Allah and Atatürk: Liberal Islam in Turkey' (2005) 9 *The International Journal of Human Rights* 307; S Langlaude, 'Indoctrination, Secularism, Religious Liberty and the ECHR' (2006) 55 *ICLQ* 929; F Tulkens, 'The European Convention on Human Rights and Church–State Relations: Pluralism vs. Pluralism' (2008) 30 *Cardozo Law Review* 2575.

54 S Wheatley, 'Democracy in International Law: A European Perspective' (2002) 51 *ICLQ* 225, 243.

55 Ibid 242–4.

Nonetheless, the conduct of the European Court in general, and local European judicial authorities seems to disregard political entities that do not constitute a direct threat to democracy. Although the verdict in *Refah Partisi* is an exception, a fair assessment should be made on the rule. There are a number of intolerant political parties within the European Union and the nations of the Council of Europe. The British National Party in the United Kingdom, alongside a number of small fascist 'nostalgic' groups in mainland Europe, are clear examples of intolerant right-wing entities.[56] However, the prospect of such parties to reach executive power in their nations is considered an unforeseen possibility and, thus, they are not considered a serious threat to the presence of the democratic society in their nations.

From the previous, one could determine that the ECtHR had a significant role in the development of the substantive right to democracy in international law. This is based on its affirmation in the inclusion of other rights with its comprehension of democracy and the democratic society. The most significant contribution however was the *Refah* principle, which formulated a democratic methodology to exclude intolerant actors. The right to democracy could have furthermore developed if the Court provided a complete list of the rights associated with democracy and the democratic society.

The role of regional organizations was effective in the development of the right to democracy in international law. It is safe to say that it surpassed the role of international organizations in that respect, due to the minimization of political and ideological conflicts that undermined the term at the international level.

3.5 Conclusion: substance or procedure?

This chapter provided a detailed illustration of the substantive right to democracy in international law. It achieved this through evaluating wider developments in international law since the end of the Cold War and its ideological complications on the establishment of the term. This was realized

56 The far-right rhetoric of the BNP is based on English exceptionalism, fascism and right-wing populism. See generally JAJ Evans, 'The Dynamics of Social Change in Radical Right-wing Populist Party Support' (2005) 3 *Comparative European Politics* 76; N Copsey, 'Changing Course or Changing Clothes? Reflections on the Ideological Evolution of the British National Party 1999–2006' (2007) 41 *Patterns of Prejudice* 61; JE Richardson, '"Our England": Discourses of "Race" and Class in Party Election Leaflets' (2008) 18 *Social Semiotics* 321. The Court has however affirmed the banning of a number of radical parties in mainland Europe on infrequent occasions: see for example *Herri Batasuna v Spain* (Apps 25803/04 & 25817/04) Judgment of the Grand Chamber of 30 June 2009.

through an assessment of international and regional organizations' instruments that contributed heavily in the redefining of the term, in addition to the role of the ECtHR in providing a richer understanding of the right to democracy in international law, beyond the thin electoral model.

However, a number of observations arise regarding the assessment of the wider substantive understanding of the right to democracy. First, nearly all post-Cold War accounts, which shaped the post-procedural understanding, did not redefine the role of the citizen, to whom the right is limited, and is the first decision maker in a democratic society. The unavailability of a legal construct that requires a limitation of the right in question – at least in terms of the right to be elected – to reasonable citizens is a conceptual problem, which cannot answer the question of political intolerance. Second, the substantive account of democracy as provided in the context of the aforementioned instruments does not directly emphasize the necessity of secularism as an essential pillar of a democratic society. Although the ECtHR stressed indirectly the issue in *Refah Partisi*, one can safely say that the *Refah* example is an exceptional case, not a rule of thumb.

An important question arises here: does the right to democracy in international law stand on the foundation of the substantive or the procedural understandings? To Gregory Fox, neither the substantive nor procedural conceptions gain dominance over one another, due to the decentralized way the issue has been addressed by international and regional organizations.[57] However, with respect to Fox's rationale, it is clear that the procedural conceptualization of the right gains dominance. This is determined not only by State practice, but also by the conduct of international organizations, where there is a general 'tendency' towards the procedural element of the right in question.[58] The assistance provided by international and regional organizations to transitional democracies has been in most circumstances in the form of procedural assistance. This has been in many cases in the form of electoral assistance and constitution writing. The most compelling examples of this are found in the conduct of the UN Electoral Assistance Division in the Department of Political Affairs that provided electoral support in a large number of cases.[59]

The UN was also involved in the direct administration of a number of territories, namely, East Timor and Kosovo, where it essentially monitored

57 Fox (n 1) paras 10, 12.
58 Burchill (n 3) 134.
59 See ND White, 'The United Nations and Democracy Assistance: Developing Practice within a Constitutional Framework' in P Burnell (ed.), *Democracy Assistance: International Co-operation for Democratization* (Psychology Press, 2002) 67, 80–1.

elections, and participated effectively in making their constitutions.[60] The Security Council recently also established a UN Support Mission in Libya, with a mandate to assist local authorities to engage in dialogue and conduct free and fair elections.[61] The mission's mandate was extended on more than one occasion, primarily, because it was focused on the procedural account of democracy, rather than the wider substantive account of the term. These are just examples of how the conduct of international organizations effectively leans towards electoral democracy. The behaviour after the conduct of an election is unfortunately ignored by international organizations, and cannot be seen as a 'triumphalism'.[62] Therefore, the position of the substantive account of the right to democracy does not reflect *lex lata* nor *lex ferenda*; rather, it should be a policy that the relevant UN and international bodies – in addition to States – should consider when enforcing democratic assistance measures.

From the previous, one could safely conclude that the understanding of democracy is not robustly distinct in international law, in both conceptualizations of the term. Both the procedural and substantive understandings of the right to democracy do not provide a complete and coherent illustration of the role of the citizen in a democratic society, and do not provide a comprehensive formula to maintain democratic governance against the threat of political intolerance. The Arab Spring failed due to the application of the procedural model, where the application of the substantive account would have led to a better result. Democracy needs to be seen as a comprehensive doctrine in its own right, and the procedure of elections is only an element in the selection of representatives. Therefore, the right to democracy in international law is still developing, and the assessment of the content and scope of the term needs to extend to its historic and philosophical origins, to complement doctrine with theory.

60 See M Ruffert, 'The Administration of Kosovo and East-Timor by the International Community' (2001) 50 *ICLQ* 613; C Stahn, 'Constitution without a State? Kosovo under the United Nations Constitutional Framework for Self-Government' (2001) 14 *Leiden Journal of International Law* 531; H Strohmeyer, 'Collapse and Reconstruction of a Judicial System: The United Nations Missions in Kosovo and East Timor' (2001) 95 *AJIL* 46; P Gorjao, 'The Legacy and Lessons of the United Nations Transitional Administration in East Timor' (2002) 24 *Contemporary Southeast Asia* 313; I Martin and A Mayer-Rieckh, 'The United Nations and East Timor: From Self-Determination to State-Building' (2005) 12 *International Peacekeeping* 125.

61 UNSC Res 2009 (16 September 2011) UN Doc S/Res/2009.

62 BR Roth, 'Evaluating Democratic Progress' in GH Fox and BR Roth (eds), *Democratic Governance and International Law* (Cambridge University Press 2000) 493, 494.

4 Democracy and the citizen in the philosophy of John Rawls

4.1 Introduction

After observing the origins of democracy in the city State of Athens, and the philosophical foundations of the social contract in the classical works of Hobbes, Locke and Rousseau, the focus of this analysis needs to extend to the contemporary understanding of democracy and the role of the citizen. The contemporary social contract tradition sets out the foundations of the modern understanding of liberal democracy. The elements and pillars of this contemporary political thought set out the grounds by which sustainable legitimate democratic governance could be maintained. The revisiting of the traditional social contract's theoretical aspects is in fact an extension of the original position(s) by which legitimacy is awarded to any form of government. The importance of this contemporary approach to this analysis is that it addresses the main issues regarding the position of democracy with regard to international law, especially, the role of the citizen in a democratic society. The importance of the main argument of assessing the role of the citizen is that he or she is the unit on which a democratic society is established and through which it is maintained. Also, international law – as this book explained earlier – confers the right to political participation on citizens only. This chapter will present John Rawls's contemporary social contract, and the theoretical framework of a democratic society.

The focus will be on John Rawls and his three major works, *A Theory of Justice*, *Political Liberalism* and *The Law of Peoples*, in addition to some reference to his paper *The Idea of Public Reason Revisited*. The reason why Rawls is central to this analysis is because he provided a framework for an instrumental right to democracy.[1] This was through his affirmation that

1 On the instrumental right to democracy as provided in the works of John Rawls, see T Christiano, 'An Instrumental Argument for a Human Right to Democracy' (2011) 39 *Philosophy & Public Affairs* 142.

democracy was to be used to achieve the principles of justice, namely, liberty. Also, the works of Rawls provide a philosophical interpretation of the *Refah* principle of reasonableness, through providing a formula for participation in the democratic process, and the exclusion of intolerant religious actors. This chapter's objective is not only to assess the Rawlsian conception of the social contact theory, but also to evaluate Rawls's moral justifications for his principles of justice that are the grounds on which other elements of his model are built.

This chapter will discuss in detail with critical evaluation the veil of ignorance theory and its relevance to the social contract and democracy. It will assess how the veil of ignorance could guarantee the application of the first and most important principle of them all, liberty. This will be followed by an assessment of Rawls's understanding of the reasonable citizen. The role of the citizen is central to this analysis, since the right to democracy and political participation is limited only to citizens. A detailed evaluation of the notions of the constitutional and overlapping consensuses will follow, since they set out the grounds of public reason, which is a core element of any democratic society. It will also discuss whether or not secularism is an important feature of democratic governance. This will be achieved through presenting a critical view of the aforementioned works and concepts.

The assessment of Rawls will inform this book through providing that the reasonable citizen, political pluralism, overlapping consensus and the other principles he advanced provide that democracy cannot be practised by those actors who have their own conception of the good, based on comprehensive religious/moral doctrines.

4.2 Liberty behind a veil of ignorance

John Rawls contributed significantly to the revival of the social contract tradition in the twentieth century. His *magnum opus* and most significant contribution to political philosophy, and what made him undoubtedly one of the most influential contemporary philosophers of his era was *A Theory of Justice*.[2]

Although the book covered a wide range of philosophical aspects, with little focus on specific ideas, it presented a codification of the unwritten

2 J Rawls, *A Theory of Justice* (revised edn, Harvard University Press 1999) (hereinafter *Theory of Justice*).

rules of liberal democracy as we see it today. *A Theory of Justice* provided Rawls's two principles of justice (which were in fact three): liberty, opportunities and income and wealth.[3] These principles were central to all of his arguments, and influenced his future publications, which will be discussed later in this chapter. This part will focus on the first principle with some reference to the other two with regard to citizenship and democracy.

The most important aspect of *A Theory of Justice* was the veil of ignorance doctrine. Rawls presented it as an essential element of liberal democracy and rational political participation. This doctrine is of significant importance to this book, and will be examined thoroughly throughout this chapter.

To begin assessing *A Theory of Justice,* one must first examine the 'original position'. Rawls revived the social contract theory, or at least revisited it, when political conditions evolved way beyond what they were centuries ago. The founders of the social contract based their theory on the state of nature, which was a hypothetical inconvenient state of lawlessness that preceded formal government, which was controlled by the desires and appetites of individual. Rawls on the other hand described the state that preceded government as 'the original position'. To Rawls 'the original position is the appropriate initial status quo which insures that the fundamental agreements reached in it are fair. This fact yields the name "justice as fairness".'[4] In order to achieve justice as provided in the Rawlsian conception of the original position, the 'principles of justice' as described earlier need to be taken into account. The most important one that is central to this assessment is the principle of liberty.

Rawls provided: 'each person is to have an equal right to the most extensive scheme of equal basic liberties compatible with a similar scheme of liberties for others'.[5] Rawls stressed that this principle stands superior to the others, where no economic and social advantages are to be gained at the expense of liberty.[6] In other words, 'liberty may only be limited for the sake of liberty'.[7] Of course, like most American philosophical doctrines, it gives property (i.e. the liberty to acquire property) a great deal. This

3 For more on the second principle, see J Rawls, 'Concepts of Distributional Equity: Some Reasons for the Maximin Criterion' (1974) 64 *The American Economic Review* 141.

4 *Theory of Justice* 15.

5 Ibid 53.

6 Ibid 54.

7 HLA Hart, 'Rawls on Liberty and Its Priority' (1973) 40 *The University of Chicago Law Review* 534. It is important to note here that Hart did not engage in assessing only *A Theory of Justice,* but also the earlier articles of Rawls.

understanding is important because it is an illustration of the modern social contract that provides the framework for an instrumental right to democracy and articulates that participants in the democratic process do not embrace a distinctive conception of the good based on a comprehensive religious or moral convection.

The doctrine looks simple at first glance; however, it is more complex than it seems. To HLA Hart, the vagueness and generality of the term 'liberty' makes it difficult to interpret Rawls's doctrine.[8] Although Hart acknowledges that Rawls limited the term 'liberty' to the basic principles of liberty, since he made use of comments to his earlier articles, he nevertheless sees it in both accounts as vague and general.[9]

However, it is important to allow such general terms when it comes to the basic principles of liberty. Vagueness widens the scope of freedoms, which is important for the development of the democratic society. Also, societies evolve, and values are not the same in one place and another. Therefore, a specific list of basic liberties will not allow this doctrine to stand the test of time.

Further, when it comes to choosing between conflicting liberties, Hart recognizes Rawls's criteria of rationalism, where a rational decision is to be made on which liberty to choose. However, Hart asserts:

> I do not understand how they can make a rational decision, in terms of self-interest, to have the various liberties at the cost of their general distribution. Opting for the most extensive liberty for all cannot, I think, be presented as always being the best insurance against the worst in conditions of uncertainty about one's own temperament and desires.[10]

It is true that Rawls did not engage in depth with the issue of human desires and appetites. Perhaps, because his writings show that unlike the founders of the social contract theory, he did not have an interest in anthropology. The point Hart elevated thereof is nevertheless a valid one; however, it is an issue of opinion and does not have a definitive answer. Rationalism as Rawls stressed 'is the standard one familiar in social theory';[11] hence, other aspects are a matter of debate.

8 Ibid 536.

9 Ibid 539.

10 Ibid 551. For more critique on the Rawlsian principle of liberty, see B Barry, 'John Rawls and the Priority of Liberty' (1973) 2 *Philosophy & Public Affairs* 274; JM Buchannan, 'The Justice of Natural Liberty' (1978) 5 *Journal of Legal Studies* 1; P De Marneffe, 'Liberalism, Liberty and Neutrality' (1990) 19 *Philosophy & Public Affairs* 253.

11 *Theory of Justice* 124.

Nagel on the other hand supports Rawls's conception of liberty. He emphasizes that '"liberalism" means different things to different people', where leftist groups and their right-wing opponents have used the term to support their own doctrines and ideologies.[12] Nonetheless, Rawls's incorporation of the term with social justice is an in-depth creation of a sound philosophical outline that extends the original ideas of liberalism as provided in the works of Locke and Kant.[13] Hence, this wide conception of liberty cannot be seen or interpreted beyond its social construct.

Therefore, a critique on the vagueness of liberty as provided in Rawls's literature could not be endorsed when the best practice of application and interpretation of democratic rights should be based on the virtue of abstract and ambiguous terms. The issue of application of democratic theory in the view of this book should be universal only to the extent of its essentials, including the pillar of liberty. After all, as mentioned earlier in this book, liberty was also an essential ingredient of the Athenian system as provided in Aristotle's work. However, with regard to the application of the details and elements of such core democratic principles, a sense of vagueness could provide a margin of appreciation. This is essential to transitional democracies and systems based on distinctive cultural and social attributes.

Also, the instrumental right to democracy in this context recognizes the value of liberty as its end. Participation in the democratic process is aimed at achieving this principle. The whole moral aspect of this hypothesis is based on liberty that should be widened by confining it to abstract terms. This cannot be achieved sustainably when the notion is limited to a certain setting based on an ideological conviction. Therefore, an overlapping consensus cannot be achieved between various *reasonable* groups when the main objective of their political participation was based on a narrow philosophical idea.

Moreover, Rawls's conception of liberty is not to be taken outside the scope of its relation to justice. After all, it was a major issue in a book called *A Theory of Justice*. In this respect, William A. Parent commented on this issue right after the book was published.[14] He asserts that Rawls was mistaken in considering the influence arising from social pressure and public opinion as constraints that limit one's liberty.[15] He argues that such pressure may constrain one's will, but certainly not one's liberty.[16] The response to

12 T Nagel, 'Rawls and Liberalism' in SR Freeman (ed.), *The Cambridge Companion to Rawls* (Cambridge University Press 2003) 62.

13 Ibid 63–4.

14 WA Parent, 'Some Recent Work on the Concept of Liberty' (1974) 11 *American Philosophical Quarterly* 166.

15 Ibid.

16 Ibid.

Parent's argument is that popular sovereignty is all about public opinion. Societies had evolved from absolutism. If the public wears a veil of ignorance and makes legitimate and rational claims, it is entitled to it, even at the expense of liberty.

The veil of ignorance that was mentioned in the previous paragraph is indeed Rawls's most important philosophical contribution. Although he was not the first to come up with the idea, nor was he the first to use the term, he definitely was the first to use it in this context.[17] A political society could never encounter the problems of minority rights, or the threat of the tyranny of the majority when applying the veil of ignorance theory.

This was indeed the first foundation of the veil of ignorance theory, which is seen as an essential prerequisite for the establishment of a democratic society. Rawls's account of the theory may be best summarized in his own words:

> Somehow we must nullify the effects of special contingences which put men at odds and tempt them to exploit social and natural circumstances to their own advantage. Now in order to do this I assume that the parties are situated behind a veil of ignorance. They do not know how the various alternatives will affect their own particular case and they are obliged to evaluate principles solely on the basis of general considerations.[18]

Rawls hypothesizes that the architecture of the social political order is based on the ignorance of the final outcome of the individual. The subject of the veil of ignorance does not take into account his race, ethnicity, language, religion, gender, class, income or any other aspect that gives one a special character or advantage. Therefore, with ignorance, one has no knowledge of his final outcome in society, and he/she will only then be in a position to make a genuine rational decision based on the position of the most disadvantaged member of society (minimax principle).[19]

The necessity of the veil of ignorance is vital for the establishment of a sustainable democratic society. Therefore, without ignorance, citizens who

17 The term was first used by JC Harsanyi in his paper 'Cardinal Utility in Welfare Economics and in the Theory of Risk-taking' (1953) 61 *Journal of Political Economy* 434, 435. It is important to note here that Rawls acknowledged that Harsanyi 'used a similar idea' in *Concepts of Distributional Equity* (n 3) 141.

18 *Theory of Justice* 118.

19 For a critical view on the minimax principle, see N Frohlich, JA Oppenheimer and CL Eavey, 'Choices of Principles of Distributive Justice in Experimental Groups' (1987) 31 *American Journal of Political Science* 606.

compose together the democratic society become biased to their own communities. In other words, every individual will favour his own sectarian or ethnic entity over the best interest of the commonwealth. However, when individuals have no knowledge of the person they will turn out to be in the final outcome, a fair political order can be designed based on the benefit of the most disadvantaged individual. When the veil of ignorance is applied, not only is a reasonable and sustainable democratic society established, but it will also come with justice and fairness.

Moreover, the veil of ignorance theory cannot be effective and useful for democracy unless it is implemented on decision makers. In a democratic society, citizens are the first decision makers, since they elect their legislators who adopt laws and monitor their enforcement, subject to the form of the democratic system applied. However, it is important to have 'veil rules' in the constitution in order to guarantee the enforcement of such laws in the benefit of the most disadvantaged individual in society, in a way that best serves the political order. Such rules '[suppress] self-interested decisionmaking by introducing uncertainty about who the beneficiary of a decision will be. Conflict rules, roughly speaking, proceed by making the decisionmaker certain that he will not be the beneficiary.'[20] Therefore constitutional provisions which provide a separation or balance of powers between the traditional branches of government are indeed veil rules, since they guarantee that no branch will gain any benefit over the other, based on pre-set rules which all stake holders have known prior to the date which they assumed office.

The veil of ignorance therefore is the prerequisite not for democracy (narrowly defined), but for its end, justice. Liberty (however defined) cannot be achieved without the establishment of a democratic society through a system of cooperation over generations. The final aim and goal of such society is to maintain liberty as a principle of justice. Behind a veil of ignorance, democracy evolves from mere periodic elections to a tool of justice; from a form of government to a mirror of legitimacy; from a constitutional provision to a value. This of course cannot be achieved through only assessing decision makers, but also requires a deep evaluation of the main element of democratic governance, the citizen. However, what is the nature of the subject behind the veil? And what is the hypothetical model it applies? The answer to these questions is, simply, the reasonable citizen.

20 A Vermeule, 'Veil of Ignorance Rules in Constitutional Law' (2001) 111 *The Yale Law Journal* 405.

4.3 The reasonable citizen

After publishing his famous *A Theory of Justice*, Rawls shifted his focus to the issue of stability. He published a number of lectures in a book he called *Political Liberalism.*[21] In the beginning of *Political Liberalism*, Rawls stressed the revival of the social contract tradition through differentiating between its political and moral conceptions.[22] He clearly asserted that the notion of political liberalism limits the scope of the term to the reasonableness of justice, rather than seeing it as an unquestioned truth or goal, as this chapter considered it in his previous publications.[23] However, the whole hypothesis of *Political Liberalism* revolves around one complex question: 'How is it possible that there may exist over time a stable and just society of free and equal citizens profoundly divided by reasonable religious, philosophical, and moral doctrines?'[24] To answer this question, he revisited *A Theory of Justice* by slightly modifying his two principles of justice in a lexical manner in order to fulfill practical societal requirements. Also, he closely examined the notion of overlapping consensus and introduced the idea of public reason in his publication that will be discussed in detail later on in this section.

In order to assess the answer to Rawls's central question, one must first understand the Rawlsian social contract in the context of *Political Liberalism.* This book does not add to the original position as the state prior to government, but it describes the condition of the people party to such contract, excluding the government or monarch. To Rawls, a social contract can only be formed between reasonable citizens. Here, one must stand and stress the word *reasonable*. Also, the importance of assessing the role of the reasonable citizen is of vital importance, where he/she is the subject of the instrumental right to democracy. To Rawls, citizenship is not a mere legal condition between an individual and a State, under which he becomes a member in its entity and enjoys its protection, but a value that comes with many duties towards other individuals. In his own words:

> Citizens are reasonable when, viewing one another as free and equal in a system of cooperation over generations, they are prepared to offer one another fair terms of social cooperation . . . and they agree to act on those terms, even at the cost of their own interests in particu-

21 J Rawls, *Political Liberalism* (expanded edn, Columbia University Press 2005) (hereinafter *Political Liberalism*).

22 Ibid xv.

23 Ibid xx.

24 Ibid xxv.

> lar situations, provided that others also accept those terms. For those terms to be fair terms, citizens offering them must reasonably think that those citizens to whom they are offered might also reasonably accept them. . . . They must be able to do this as free and equal, and not as dominated or manipulated, or under the pressure of an inferior political or social position.[25]

The key questions that arise here are: who is the citizen that Rawls considers *reasonable*? And what are the characteristics of such categorization?

In order to answer the previous questions, one may observe from the above passage that, to Rawls, reasonableness is the most important element of citizenship in its democratic sense. Such reasonableness is realized when a democratic society is created through the cooperation of its individual elements, the citizens. However, such cooperation cannot be realized when citizens are influenced and pressured by any other political position. Such position is based on comprehensive doctrines, whether they were based on a religious, moral, philosophical or ideological conception of the good.

This conception calls for a reflection. It has a romantic sense and a Utopian view. However, it is more than that. Reasonable citizenship is the main pillar of democracy. It is built on the condition that such citizens are to be free and equal, and this indeed is a condition that cannot be applied in a non-democratic society. It also requires that the State that sponsors such citizens have a legislative and executive regime that respects and protects fundamental human rights, accompanied with a popular culture of pluralism and deliberation. Further, legislative measures are not enough to eliminate inequalities. All forms of inequality need to be removed, or at least minimized behind a veil of ignorance in accordance with Rawls's second principle of justice – thus, providing equal opportunities to citizens helps them make rational decisions.

Also, reasonable citizenship requires the application of Rawls's most significant doctrine, the veil of ignorance. This doctrine needs to be applied by decision makers as elaborated earlier, but it equally needs to be applied by citizens themselves, not as a constitutional provision, but as a value and belief. One can only be reasonable when one puts oneself in the position of the most disadvantaged individual before making a decision. Only then is such decision deemed to be rational, and the citizen who makes it a rational citizen.

Furthermore, in order to achieve such aspirations, no 'inferior' pressure is to be practised on them. This term also calls for elaboration. In the view of

25 Ibid xliv, 49 and 54.

this study, Rawls meant by this statement that citizenship, as a romantic concept, is superior to all other affiliations. One's loyalty to one's nation holds greater value than all others. Therefore, contradicting loyalties between one's nation and one's political ideology, religion or ethnicity is not found in reasonable citizens, given that the preconditions of freedom and equality are provided.

Citizens are at the end of the day as individuals the units that form society. With reasonable citizens we get a reasonable society.[26] Rawls's approach in this sense was to achieve a rational society as an end or goal through citizens who found it not only ideal, but also necessary. However, not only rational citizens form what Rawls calls a 'well-ordered democratic society'. According to Rawls, such society is based on everyone's acceptance of the two principles of justice, a system of cooperation between society's political and social institutions, and citizens' compliance with such institutions.[27] He differentiates between the well-ordered democratic society and a community or association through affirming that it is a 'complete and closed social system';[28] complete in the sense that it possesses all the necessary means of human life, and closed since one enters it at birth leaves it by death, and no one has any affiliation or identity before becoming a member of such society.[29]

Thus, the Rawlsian account of citizenship supplements international law's incomplete understanding of the term, through requiring the condition of reasonableness for political participation. It does therefore compliment the *Refah* principle of reasonableness that is necessary to maintain democracy, and provides an efficient answer to political intolerance and the necessity to protect democracy against competing comprehensive doctrines and alternative ideologies. Therefore, the instrumental right to democracy that aims to use the notion to provide a number of objectives in the sphere of justice requires one to prioritize the affiliation to society over any other religious and moral connection.

4.4 The overlapping consensus

In addition to setting out the theoretical framework of his three principles of justice and his conception of citizenship, Rawls answered the question of diversity in society through the application of a number of political

26 It is important to note here that Rawls makes a big distinction between the reasonable and the rational, but it is not, in the view of this book, central to his argument. See *Political Liberalism* 48–54.

27 Ibid 35.

28 Ibid 40.

29 Ibid 40–1.

doctrines. The notion of 'overlapping consensus' is the most compelling one with regard to his main arguments. He introduced the notion after affirming that society is built on diversity, where not all citizens affirm any single comprehensive religious, moral or rational doctrine. Therefore 'citizens who affirm reasonable but opposing comprehensive doctrines belong to an overlapping consensus: that is, they generally endorse that conception of justice as giving the content of their political judgements on basic institutions; and second, unreasonable comprehensive doctrines. . . do not gain enough currency to undermine society's essential justice.'[30]

From this, one learns that, to Rawls, achieving stability with a sustainable social structure can only be achieved through an overlapping consensus.[31] Such consensus needs to be between reasonable political and ideological doctrines.[32] Thus, excluding religious and political actors, with unreasonable and irrational doctrines, is not only justified, but necessary to achieve an overlapping consensus. The aim of this consensus should be focused on establishing justice, as an independent conception, within the scope of the two principles, and unattached to any political or religious ideology.[33] Therefore, the idea of the overlapping consensus is an essential element to the instrumental right to democracy. This is because it extends the idea of reasonableness to the participants in the democratic process at the decision-making level. It also provides a rationale for the exclusion of intolerant actors, and a philosophical interpretation of the *Refah* principle. However, a prerequisite for founding an overlapping consensus is the establishment of constitutional consensus first.

In order to found a constitutional consensus, a constitution that satisfies the principles of a liberal democracy needs to be established, in order to regulate legitimate rivalry in the political arena.[34] Such constitution incorporates a number of provisions that protect and promote justice as an end behind, of course, a veil of ignorance. Even if citizens did not find the constitution, and the provisions of justice thereof, similar to their own ideological or moral beliefs, they will see them as superior. After all, as explained earlier, one of the main pillars of the well-ordered democratic society is that citizens respect their political institutions, and the constitution in this respect is the founder of all legitimate political entities. Hence, all recognized political actors, and citizens thereof, submit to the constitution before

30 Ibid 38–9.
31 Ibid 43.
32 Ibid 144.
33 Ibid.
34 Ibid 158.

submitting to their own conceptions. Therefore, those who have a political doctrine that holds an alternative system to democratic governance are indeed unreasonable and are not subject to the constitutional consensus to start with, so they are party to the overlapping consensus. Also, this cannot be achieved unless the constitution was adopted democratically, through a constituent assembly or referendum, or through any other method recognized in a democratic society.[35]

Once the constitutional consensus is established, political groups of various ideological orientations need to enter into dialogue with each other in order to found similar grounds of understanding, in light of the principles of justice upon which the constitutional consensus was established.[36] Excluding intolerant actors, who do not support liberal democracy as a form of government, should be already established at this stage, since they do not support the fundamental grounds of the Rawlsian contract and liberal constitutional regime. After having such dialogue, with time and practice, a popular culture of liberal democracy is founded in society, the well-ordered democratic society that is, which is the source of all legitimacy, and the subject of the constitutional and overlapping consensus.

Therefore, an overlapping consensus is when rival political groups, with conflicting interests and ideologies agree to and support liberal democratic principles, under a democratic constitutional regime in order to achieve justice.[37] However, although it is called a consensus, it does not necessarily need to include the approval of each and every political actor. That is because in politics it is very difficult – if not impossible – to find agreement between everyone. In the view of this book, the consensus here is established between the most active political actors, provided that they do not adopt an intolerant ideology, believe in the spirit of their nation's constitution and include the fundamental pillars of liberal democracy in their political manifestos.[38] Also, it needs to be founded through a considerable period of time, in order to establish a popular culture that supports such principles

35 For a critique on the Rawlsian notion of a constitutional consensus, see generally SS Wolin, 'The Liberal/Democratic Divide on Rawls's *Political Liberalism*' (1996) 24 *Political Theory* 97; C Mouffe, 'The Limits of John Rawls's Pluralism' (2005) 4 *Politics, Philosophy & Economics* 221; DP Dauenhauer, 'A Good Word for a Modus Vivendi' in V Davion and C Wolf (eds), *The Idea of Political Pluralism: Essays on Rawls* (Rowman & Littlefield 2000) 204.

36 *Political Liberalism* 165.

37 Ibid 168.

38 It is important to note here that the desire to amend the constitution does not violate the constitutional consensus, as long as it does not replace the democratic system with an alternative form of governance.

in order to found a popular consensus to ensure its sustainability, stability and continuation throughout generations.

4.5 Public reason

Another important political doctrine in the contemporary social contract is the idea of public reason, originally found in Immanuel Kant's piece *What is Enlightenment*.[39] Kant argued that the public use of reason was necessary to improve the private function of individuals. He gives examples of public reason 'a scholar addressing the real public through his writings, the clergyman making public use of his reason enjoys unlimited freedom to use his own reason and to speak in his own person'.[40] In other words, public reasoning is basically when individuals openly deliberate on issues that concern the public. Therefore, it excludes issues that only concern a certain group, whether it was an ethnic, linguistic or religious minority, or any other group of people with a common interest. Rawls on the other hand developed the idea in *Political Liberalism*. He discussed the idea with a lot of detail; however, for the purpose of this book, the focus will only be on its scope and nature, and its relation to religion and citizenship.

In the view of this study, the conception of public reason provides a theoretical reflection of the *Refah* principle of reasonableness which is necessary for the maintenance of democracy. This is founded on the fact that it encompasses an equitable restriction on the practice of political rights – not limited to the right to vote and to be elected – based on the main pillar of the Rawlsian theory, reason. Therefore, when applied with other aspects of the contemporary social contract (overlapping consensus, veil of ignorance and liberty) democracy is extended beyond its limited procedural understanding to incorporate the institutional methods necessary for its sustainable success.

To Rawls, public reason is the product of 'reasonable' pluralism.[41] It is only imagined capable of succeeding in a 'well-ordered constitutional democratic society', where a culture of free institutions allows the presence of conflicting ideological, religious and political doctrines, on the condition, that is, that they are reasonable.[42] Rawls stresses that unreasonable comprehensive doctrines that are incompatible with the foundations of democracy

39 I Kant, 'An Answer to the Question: What Is Enlightenment?' in HS Reiss (ed.), *Kant: Political Writings* (Cambridge University Press 1970).

40 Ibid 57.

41 *Political Liberalism* 441.

42 Ibid 440–1.

are to be excluded from public reasoning.[43] This approach certainly makes sense, since it is theoretically impossible to reason with the unreasonable.

The objective of public reason as this book understands it – since Rawls does not explicitly say it in any of his writings – is to achieve justice according to Rawls's two principles.[44] It is not a mere debate in order to prove certain moral truths or philosophical positions, rather an open forum of reasonable discussion. Each person who reasons publicly must keep in mind that the final outcome should be in favour of liberty, income and opportunities. Individual views that favour liberty, for instance, vary in terms of how it shall be executed, enforced and protected. The content of such discussion is in current or on-going political and social affairs which one finds in the media or in any other credible source of information.

The subject of public reason meanwhile is reasonable citizens. When citizens deliberate on matters of concern in a well-ordered democratic society, a deliberative democracy emerges. The two significant factors of such a form of democracy are public reason and the desire of citizens to follow public reason and apply its outcome in their political behaviour. However, Rawls stresses that in order to realize such outcome, a society needs to be not only a well-ordered democratic one within a constitutional framework, but also an educated society.[45] The requirement of an education is a logical condition in order for citizens to make legitimate decisions through their knowledge of the content of their debate. Knowledge of the constitutional system requires civic education, and knowledge of current affairs requires free media, both of which are features of a modern democracy.

Further, in *The Idea of Public Reason Revisited* Rawls certainly presented the most important question in contemporary democratic thought: 'Can democracy and comprehensive doctrines, religious or nonreligious, be compatible?'[46] To answer this, a comprehensive religious doctrine, under the authority of a Church, or a *marja'a*, clearly does not favour a system of constitutional democratic governance.[47] The religious and moral values of such institutions endorse a certain conception of justice, which conflicts with the principles of Political Liberalism. Only reasonable comprehensive doctrines could function in a democratic society, even if they had a religious

43 Ibid 441–2.

44 He does not explicitly say it that way, however it is understood in the context of his view on the content of public reason. See *Political Liberalism* 450–8.

45 Ibid 449.

46 J Rawls, *The Law of Peoples: With the Idea of Public Reason Revisited* (Harvard University Press 2001) (hereinafter *Law of Peoples*) 175.

47 Ibid.

background.[48] Such doctrines are seen as reasonable in this context if they do not reject the basic features of a constitutional democracy.[49]

In the same paper, Rawls makes an important assertion in order to distinguish between public reason and secular reason and values.[50] To Rawls, secular reason is between 'comprehensive nonreligious doctrines'. He continues to assert that a political doctrine by and large does not reflect moral values.[51] On the other hand, moral and religious values are comprehensive with their own conception of the good. A secular argument that contradicts a religious one on the basis of opposing principles is a moral one, not political.[52] Therefore, both arguments are not subject to public reason because of their moral nature.

As for religion and public reason in a democratic society, it is important to acknowledge that it would be considered difficult to reconcile those who endorse faith and religion and the secularists who hold no religious doctrine in a constitutional regime. The solution to this conflicting situation is simply through toleration.[53] It is not to be seen as different to any other case of conflicting comprehensive doctrines. Basically, when there is a constitutional consensus, followed by the establishment of a well-ordered democratic society, which is formed by reasonable citizens, any conflict is between reasonable individuals. Extra toleration is perhaps needed in this case, since one of the conflicting doctrines wants to achieve a moral truth or victory; however, it is not indeed to be achieved at the expense of democracy since, as explained earlier, it will be seen as an unreasonable doctrine which is incompatible with democracy and, thus, is excluded from public reasoning. The same rule applies to unreasonable secularists and any faction of society that holds views incompatible with democracy.

The key lesson from the principle of public reason and the general elements of Rawls's thesis with regard to the instrumental right to democracy is that according to the contemporary social contract, citizens are reasonable, which makes them open to the reasonable ideas of others. This is fundamental in the establishment and maintenance of a democratic society and acts as a philosophical interpretation of the *Refah* principle. Therefore, those who encompass a distinctive conception of the good, based on a comprehensive religious doctrine, and do not use democracy as a means to enforce other

48 Ibid 177.
49 Ibid.
50 *Political Liberalism* 452.
51 Ibid.
52 Ibid 457–8.
53 Ibid 461.

rights and freedoms, cannot participate in the democratic process for their failure to consent to reasonableness.

4.6 An escape from liberty

The Law of Peoples is one of John Rawls's most compelling and controversial publications, which has a great relevance to this thesis.[54] It was first published in a short paper under the same title in 1993.[55] The book was published after the original paper was extended and merged with *The Idea of Public Reason Revisited* in 1999.[56] He states in the beginning of *The Law of Peoples* that he used the term *peoples* instead of *nations* in order to use a wider horizon beyond the traditional construct of sovereign entities.[57] It is clearly not a book written by an international lawyer; however, it is of significant value to international lawyers when observing the critical philosophical aspects of international law provided in its text, especially that its philosophical approach was to extend the contemporary social contract tradition, through the idea of Justice as Fairness to the wider Society of Peoples.[58] This section will provide a reverse view of *The Law of Peoples* through critically assessing what this book views as Rawls's escape from liberalism, driven from the standpoint that Rawls originally used to defend his abstract understanding of liberty in his debate with HLA Hart as provided earlier in this chapter, and the effects this approach has on the instrumental right to democracy.

Rawls, as an American philosopher, was focused on the domestic. His previous major works were dedicated to the enforcement of justice in a liberal democracy. To achieve that, he came with the hypothesis of the original position, the veil of ignorance doctrine and, of course, the role of the citizen in a democratic society. *The Law of Peoples* on the other hand is Rawls's first major work dedicated to the enforcement of his theory at an international level. For this purpose, the original position was modified, and the veil of ignorance became thinner and more flexible.

54 *Law of Peoples* (n 46).
55 J Rawls, 'The Law of Peoples' (1993) 20 *Critical Inquiry* 36.
56 J Rawls, 'The Idea of Public Reason Revisited' (1997) 64 *The University of Chicago Law Review* 765. It is important to note here that the paper was also added to *Political Liberalism* in its expanded edition.
57 *Law of Peoples* v.
58 Ibid vi, 2.

Rawls starts *The Law of Peoples* by focusing on two kinds of internal governments that may either be liberal democracies or non-liberal but decent polities.[59] This categorization is central to his argument, and very relevant to this book, which mainly focuses on the application of the democratic norm in international law to Arab (Muslim) political societies. For this, he presents a case study on a decent government (Kazanistan) that has many similar attributes to the States subject to the focus of this book.[60] Further, he also categorizes the domestic societies of peoples as reasonable liberal peoples, decent peoples, outlaw states, societies burdened by unfavorable conditions and benevolent absolutisms. This categorization of peoples is of equal importance to this thesis, since one cannot apply the social contract without fully understanding both parties to the contract, which are the government and the governed, whether it was in its traditional or contemporary sense.

The first issue of assessment will be why Rawls focused on peoples instead of nations in his hypothesis? The answer to this question is based on three fundamental aspects: the basic features of peoples, the basic feature of States and the concept of sovereignty. Based on his account that members of liberal democratic societies are by large the subject of the law of peoples, Rawls suggests that such peoples have the following features: 'a reasonably just constitutional democratic government that serves their fundamental interests; citizens united by. . . "common sympathies"; and finally, a moral nature'.[61] The first institutional feature suggests by default that government is controlled by the electoral will of the people, and has no interest or objective other than protecting their freedom and interests, independent from conflicting influences by private economic powers.[62] The second feature holds a cultural nature. Being united by democratic governance and common sympathies, which have a lingual or historical nature, is essential to build political principles.[63] Finally, the moral feature requires citizens to be both reasonable and rational in order to work in system of cooperation over generations behind a veil of ignorance, as explained earlier in Rawls's theory of Justice as Fairness.[64] The three features create collectively the concept of sovereignty as stipulated in *The Law of Peoples* as a cosmopolitan

59 Ibid 1.
60 Kazanistan is a fictional Muslim nation, not to be confused with the Republic of Kazakhstan.
61 *Law of Peoples* 23.
62 Ibid 24.
63 Ibid 24–5.
64 Ibid 25.

one, rather than the classic understanding of the term provided by cynical international legal theorists.[65]

James Crawford has another view on the issue of *peoples* and governments with regard to global governance and international legal theory. In his paper 'The Rights of Peoples: "Peoples" or "Governments"?' he makes a number of remarks on the subject of international law.[66] First, that the units of international law are States, and thus, it is a law of *States* rather than the units that involve them, *peoples*. Second, that international law provides decisive answers to addressing rights, while in philosophy, the issue of *rights* is very problematic, and cannot be constrained to universal definitions.[67]

It is clear that Crawford provides an international lawyer's perspective, while Rawls's approach is anything but a legal one. As mentioned earlier, Rawls is clearly not an international lawyer, and he certainly did not claim to be one; however, his approach comes strictly from a political and theoretical point of view that he stated clearly in his debate with Habermas. The limitation to this discipline continues to *The Law of Peoples*. However, the whole issue of rights cannot be limited to the discipline of international law. The entire purpose of the protection of individual freedoms and fundamental rights requires the involvement of all relevant disciplines.

Rawls undoubtedly takes Crawford's argument – and mainstream international legal theory – to another level. Instead of viewing States as the units of international law, Rawls's theory is based on citizens – peoples – of such States. Rawls's theoretical viewpoint comes from a grassroots perspective that constitutes a critical view of the classic understanding of sovereignty in international legal theory. To Rawls, traditional sovereignty provides autonomy to a nation in all affairs regarding its people.[68] Such autonomy is strongly rejected by Rawls on the basis that a State may not have full internal sovereignty on its citizens on the issue of human rights.[69] There are many details Rawls chose not to engage in; however, it is safe to say that international law has evolved beyond the traditional conception of

65 D Held, 'Law of States, Law of Peoples: Three Models of Sovereignty' (2002) 8 *Legal Theory* 1, 3. On the rejection of cosmopolitan sovereignty, see S Smith, 'Reasons of State' in D Held and C Pollitt (eds), *New Forms of Democracy* (Sage 1987); KJ Holsti, *International Politics: A Framework of Analysis* (5th edn, Englewood Cliffs 1988); B Buzan, R Little and C Jones, *The Logic of Anarchy* (Columbia University Press 1993).

66 J Crawford, 'The Rights of Peoples: "Peoples" or "Governments"?' (1985) 9 *Bulletin of the Australian Society of Legal Philosophy* 136.

67 Ibid.

68 Ibid 25–6.

69 Ibid 27.

sovereignty.[70] But nevertheless, Rawls's concern and rejection of the notion is highly justified, based on his lenience towards the progressive notion of cosmopolitan sovereignty.

The main objective of *The Law of Peoples* is to demonstrate 'how the content of a Law of Peoples might be developed out of a liberal idea of justice similar to, but more general than, the idea [of] justice as fairness'.[71] In other words, it applies the theory of justice as fairness on a wider international level, rather than its original limitation to domestic political societies. This part will evaluate this ambitious objective through assessing the principles of the conception of *The Law of Peoples*.

The original position is originally a hypothetical model where the liberal people (on a domestic/national level) are represented by rational representatives who make decisions behind a veil of ignorance, where representatives are unaware of the people's individual conception of the good. A second original position is what Rawls is suggesting to extend the social contract to an international level.[72] It also involves rational representatives of reasonable liberal peoples behind a veil of ignorance. However, it is altered, where the veil of ignorance is adjusted to incorporate the different scale of representation involved. This may include the representative's unawareness of the territory or population of the people they represent; however, they need to be aware of the favourable conditions which make liberal democracy succeed.[73]

On examining the second original position, one can find that it is based in both cases on a thick veil of ignorance. A thick veil of ignorance is not only expected at the domestic level, but also necessary for the establishment of a sustainable liberal democratic society beyond constitutional provisions and legislation. However, at an international level, one may expect a thinner veil. Flexibility is needed in international relations, and favourable conditions may not be the same from one place to another; in fact, they might even contradict, which makes such representation difficult if not impossible. Also, the aim of this second original position is to arrange cooperation between peoples who come from different nations and have various political, social and historical backgrounds and have different interests.

70 See A Buchanan, 'Rawls's Law of Peoples: Rules for a Vanished Westphalian World' (2000) 110 *Ethics* 697. For more on contemporary accounts on sovereignty, see generally L Gross, 'The Peace of Westphalia' (1948) 42 *AJIL* 20; J Bartelson, 'The Concept of Sovereignty Revisited' (2006) 17 *EJIL* 463; DJ Bederman, *Globalization and International Law* (Palgrave MacMillan 2008).

71 *Law of Peoples* 3.

72 Ibid 32.

73 Ibid 32–3.

Even though they were all from well-ordered democratic societies and had a longstanding liberal-democratic culture; a conflict of interest is inevitable. Therefore, a thinner veil of ignorance is necessary in order to realistically apply the Law of Peoples.

Further, Rawls expressed *The Law of Peoples* as a realistic Utopia. This comes from an angle that reconciles political idealism with practical political and social conditions.[74] This is realized through Rawls's classic notion of reasonable citizenship, as he expressed: 'The idea of a reasonably just society of well-ordered peoples will not have an important place in a theory of international politics until such peoples exist and have learned to coordinate the actions of their governments in wider forms of political, economic, and social cooperation.'[75] This is an extension of the original argument Rawls provided in *Political Liberalism* as this chapter discussed earlier in detail.

The importance of reasonable citizenship in this context is in the fact that citizens are the subject of the Law of Peoples. Beyond the various categorizations of peoples which Rawls provided, and the numerous requirements of a realistic Utopia, reasonableness is the most striking and relevant. The main characteristics of reasonable citizens are: 'First, they stand ready to offer fair terms of social cooperation between equals, and they abide by these terms if others do so, even should it be to their advantage or not; second, reasonable persons recognize and accept the consequences of the burdens of judgement, which leads to the idea of reasonable toleration in a democratic society.'[76] However, an important question arises on the application of the reasonableness requirement at a wider, international level.

The answer to this question lies in the toleration of non-liberal peoples. According to Rawls, there is no problem in the application of the Law of Peoples to the well-ordered liberal democratic peoples of the world. However, they are only a part, if not a small part, of the Society of Peoples. Therefore, it is important to extend the Law of Peoples, through extending the reasonableness it requires to include toleration.[77]

To Rawls, toleration in this context is 'to recognise that these nonliberal societies as equal participating members good standing of the Society of Peoples, with certain rights and obligations, including the duty of civility requiring that they offer other peoples public reasons appropriate to the

74 Ibid 11.
75 Ibid 19.
76 Ibid 177.
77 Ibid 59.

Society of Peoples for their actions.' Toleration is after all one of the basic principles of liberalism.[78]

The non-liberal peoples to whom Rawls's Law of Peoples is extended are decent hierarchical peoples. By this, outlaw states and societies burdened by unfavourable conditions are excluded from the Law of Peoples,[79] and therefore will not be the focus of this analysis. The conditions of categorizing peoples as decent and hierarchical include that they do not have aggressive means to achieve legitimate ends, and have a civilized and sophisticated legal system.[80]

A non-liberal but decent hierarchical people have a number of characteristics that distinguish them from their well-ordered liberal counterparts. A decent society is not as reasonable as a liberal one.[81] However, although it does not provide reasonable representation to its citizens at a domestic level, and applies instead a system of hierarchal consultation, it applies the principle of the Law of Peoples reasonably.[82] What makes such societies decent is that they 'have a common good political conception of justice, and this conception is honored in its decent consultation hierarchy'.[83] The extent to which decent societies respect the Law of Peoples is equal to their liberal fellows.[84]

Further, a decent society may acquire comprehensive philosophical or religious doctrines. These doctrines do not violate the Law of Peoples as long as they do not unreasonably limit fundamental liberties.[85] Rawls elaborated on this by using the fictitious Muslim State of Kazanistan as an example.[86] Kazanistan does not separate church from State, where only believers of the State religion could influence government policies, including foreign affairs. However, it tolerates minority groups in a system of cooperation, and fundamental freedoms are not unreasonably oppressed. Also, a system of consultation is provided in governance, although it does not fit the liberal criteria of reasonable representation as explained earlier.

78 See J Locke, *A Letter Concerning Toleration* (first published 1685, Hacket Publishers 1983).
79 *Law of Peoples* 63.
80 Ibid 64–5.
81 Ibid 83.
82 Ibid 71–5, 83
83 Ibid 83.
84 Ibid.
85 Ibid 74.
86 Ibid 74–8.

This position has been opposed by many critics, and indeed portrayed as treachery of liberalism.[87] The strongest opposition was by Kok-Chor Tan.[88] Tan believed in a comprehensive liberal approach, both at a domestic and international level. He argued that States needed to extend liberalism not only to the political participation of their citizens, but also to other aspects of their lives.[89] On the international level, Tan strongly advocated the protection of human rights, with no toleration for States who restricted the fundamental rights of their citizens.[90] Therefore, decent States cannot be part of this international system of cooperation since they violate the basic principles of comprehensive liberalism.[91]

Tan's critique is based on the democratic pillar of toleration. Pluralism and acceptance are essential ingredients of a democratic society and Rawls has affirmed this in his domestic theory. However, his toleration of non-liberal societies in his expanded international model cannot be accepted in the name of realism.[92] To Tan this is a serious fault in *The Law of Peoples*.[93] It is a compromise rather than a licit philosophical doctrine.

Fernando Tesón agrees with Tan's critique on *The Law of Peoples*.[94] He believes that Rawls's conception of liberalism should extend to all peoples rather than be conceded to fulfill international political considerations. The settlements and extended toleration Rawls advances fail to achieve the basic moral benchmarks of the international order, where liberal tolerance cannot be forgiving of violations to essential human rights and fundamental freedoms.

Further, Allan Buchanan also made a number of valid observations on *The Law of Peoples*, paying particular attention to Rawls's 'betrayal of liberalism'.[95] To Buchanan, the main problem finds its roots in the basics of Rawls's theory of peoples. There is no doubt that recent scholarly literature departs from the classic Westphalian understanding of sovereignty

87 See for example D Moellendorf, 'Constructing the Law of Peoples' (1996) 77 *Pacific Philosophical Quarterly* 132; FR Tesón, *A Philosophy of International Law* (Westview 1998), chap. 4.

88 KC Tan, *Toleration, Diversity, and Global Justice* (Pennsylvania State University Press 2000).

89 Ibid 49.

90 Ibid 79.

91 For more on the Tan-Rawls comparison, see C Jones, 'Global Liberalism: Political of Comprehensive' (2004) 54 *University of Toronto Law Journal* 227.

92 KC Tan, 'Liberal Toleration in Rawls's Law of Peoples' (1998) 108 *Ethics* 276.

93 Ibid 284.

94 FR Tesón, 'The Rawlsian Theory of International Law' (1995) 9 *Ethics & International Affairs* 79.

95 Buchanan (n 70) 697.

in international law; however, the extent to which Rawls's theory reflects the viewpoint of peoples is insufficient.[96] Therefore, a fully satisfactory international law moral theory must extend to include the reality of intra-state conflict through appreciating the global basic structure, especially in its economic sense.[97] Buchanan's critique is in the core foundation of the theory of peoples.

In response to Tan, Buchanan and other critics, Rawls clearly stated that his approach was not ideal, but realistic. It is necessary to tolerate such societies in order to realistically achieve a system of international cooperation between peoples instead of nations, due to religious, political and, especially, cultural differences between the different peoples of the world. Also, Rawls's toleration approach does not tolerate violations of fundamental human rights with *jus cogens* status, such as slavery and female genital mutilation. The toleration of minimal restrictions on certain political and civil liberties by a decent hierarchy could lead to the improvement of human rights in it, through an international system of cooperation which includes by and large representatives of well-ordered liberal peoples, especially since such decent people do not have an aggressive attitude. Further, the toleration of decent non-liberal peoples might also offer the advantage of encouraging them to engage with the well-ordered liberal peoples in more significant matters, even potentially deferring to them – providing always that their acceptance of any international rule must not conflict with their pride as a people.[98]

However, from an international lawyer's perspective, one cannot compromise on basic human rights. Decent hierarchical societies are obliged to respect civil liberties, individual freedoms and other basic rights. Cultural differences and religion are not accepted as an excuse to violate binding human rights norms. Female genital mutilation and slavery for instance are not subject to the toleration Rawls called for. Yet, according to international benchmarks, restrictions on some civil and political rights are only justified when necessary in a democratic society.[99] How could this be achieved when

96 Ibid 698.

97 Ibid 703–6, 716.

98 CR Beitz, 'Rawls's Law of Peoples' (2000) 110 *Ethics* 669, 675.

99 For example, Article 21 of the ICCPR states: 'The right of peaceful assembly shall be recognized. No restrictions may be placed on the exercise of this right other than those imposed in conformity with the law and which are necessary in a democratic society in the interests of national security or public safety, public order (ordre public), the protection of public health or morals or the protection of the rights and freedoms of others.'

applied in a non-democratic society to start with? To this question Rawls did not provide a realistic answer. On the other hand, State sovereignty is not absolute when it comes to human rights. Rawls stressed this point in the beginning of *The Law of Peoples* as explained earlier. This soft position on decent hierarchical peoples comes as an unnecessary contradiction. Rawls stressed that *The Law of Peoples* was a realistic utopia. Although a lot of credit could be attached to the realistic element of his doctrine, in light of expediency and the necessity to provide a functioning international order, one cannot safely assume that the notion is remotely utopian. Realism cannot reach an ideal conclusion when the issue of the lack of full protection of all basic rights and freedoms could be a matter of compromise. This is the concern in *The Law of Peoples* and, therefore, it is indeed credibly pragmatic, but equally dystopian.

Rawls answered the question of political reasonableness and the compatibility of non-liberal peoples with a system of international cooperation between peoples in *The Law of Peoples*. The toleration of reasonable citizens in well-ordered liberal societies is necessary to incorporate their non-liberal decent counterparts for the realization of a system of governance of peoples instead of nations. However, such toleration must not be a compromise on the basic principles of liberalism, democracy and human rights. In other words, a thinner, more flexible veil of ignorance is required to achieve realistic objectives. Most of the critics of the theory – as explained earlier – failed to appreciate the realistic approach of the theory that creates a necessary small grey area in international morality. Reasonableness is necessary to achieve sustainable democratic governance over generations. The basic element of a democratic society that endorses public reasoning is the citizen, who has the right to vote and be represented rationally, behind a veil of ignorance, and beyond the various competing comprehensive religious and non-religious doctrines. Applying this system of liberal democracy internationally requires its successful application at the national level, where the Law of Peoples is applied on equals without distinction. Otherwise, it will be no more than a *realistic* aspiration. However, if liberalism was to tolerate political intolerance and religious fanaticism in the name of realism, international morality will be the subject of great disappointment and regression.

With relation to the instrumental right to democracy, one can find that the escape from liberalism provided in this context also provides an escape from the instrumental entitlement. This is because the subject and end of democratic participation is not realized, and not morally necessary on the basis of realism. This issue is problematic, where the principle of liberty should not have been compromised to achieve a pragmatic objective.

4.7 Conclusion

In assessing the social contract in its contemporary sense, one may confidently accept that it provided a modern extension to the traditional account of the theory. The philosophical framework provided in the veil of ignorance, and the principles of justice – most importantly, the principle of liberty – redefines the social contract in a more applicable sense. The works of Rawls and the principles he delivered illustrate an instrumental right to democracy. This is through using the notion to achieve liberty, which is a fundamental principle of justice. The concepts of public reason, overlapping consensus and the veil of ignorance collectively act as a philosophical interpretation of the *Refah* principle, advanced by the European Court of Human Rights, that provided a formula for the exclusion of intolerant actors on the grounds of incompatibility with democracy.

The comprehensive understanding of the citizen in this context provided a very secular and reasonable understanding, which the procedural and substantive right to democracy in international law failed to address. The significance of the idea of the citizen lies in the fact that he or she is the first decision maker in a democratic society, and the unit upon which a democratic polity is founded. In terms of international law and the right to democracy and political participation in both of its procedural and substantive accounts, the entitlement is restricted to citizens only, unlike most other rights that acquire a universal character. The social contract theory complemented the international law texts by defining the role of such citizen who participates in the political process on the pillar of reasonableness, which is not seen as a luxury, but as a vital ingredient for the sustainable success of democratic governance. This understanding is necessary for the extension of the limited procedural view of international law to include essential substantive elements for the realization of the entitlement to democratic government, and a theoretical elaboration and recognition of the *Refah* principle of reasonableness for political participation.

The objective of the instrumental right to democracy as provided in this context is liberty. Rawls's toleration of liberal shortcomings in non-Western societies as expanded in his description of a *realistic utopia* represents a contradiction to his original theory. Liberty can only be limited for the sake of liberty. Hart, who viewed his conception of the notion as too vague and ambiguous, criticized him for this. However, given that the term was used to realize a social and economic order of justice, and is the aim of the instrumental right to democracy, it is highly justified for it to be elusive. Therefore, an escape from liberty on the basis of consideration and pragmatism is an escape from the main principle of justice and a denial of the instrumental right to democracy. Also, since the whole contemporary social contract theory – in the Rawlsian account at least – is fundamentally based on the three principles of justice, there should be no room for discussion on any limitation on the core element of democratic legitimacy. In other words, the toleration of the intolerant cannot be acceptable, especially in transitional societies such as the Arab World. The achievement of democracy in its instrumental sense requires no consideration of regressive models that indorse their own conception of the good, which contradicts most – if not all – of the principles Rawls advanced in his three major works.

Further, reasonableness is the most essential ingredient of democratic government and society, and a concept, which it will be recalled, international law did not convincingly address; reason versus the favouritism of a certain conception of the good affirmed in a comprehensive ideological, moral or religious doctrine that runs counter to democracy, where this contention is at the heart of any debate about the modern conception of social contract theory. Democracy is a comprehensive doctrine in its own right and its notion of the good is the achievement of justice through liberty. Therefore, unreasonable comprehensive doctrines certainly conflict with democracy and should not be subject to the elements of democratic participation, such as public reason and the overlapping consensus.

Who, then, can participate in the democratic process? The citizen is the unit on which a political society is established. However, a democratic society's unit is a reasonable citizen. In other words, political societies (States) are composed of citizens; yet, reasonable ones constitute democratic entities. The test of reasonableness is when they see each other as equals in a system of cooperation over generations. In order to achieve this, they must have first achieved a constitutional consensus that eliminates all other moral affiliation when looking to each other as members in society. In other words, the citizen who fulfills the requirement of reasonableness is the subject of political participation, and holds an entitlement to democratic government.

Is secularism essential to the requirement of reasonableness? Although Rawls's theory is not secular in the sense that it is biased towards secular rhetoric against religious beliefs, it is indeed secular in the sense that it requires the State to be neutral between comprehensive religious and moral doctrines.[100] This reasonable neutrality reflects a sensible secular morality. For the purpose of this thesis, secular morality could be defined as a State's impartiality between reasonable political doctrines based on religious

100 M Freeman, 'The Problem of Secularism in Human Rights Theory' (2004) 26 *HRQ* 375, 396.

foundations. This requires a hypothesis by which an overlapping consensus was established between reasonable political actors, even if their political doctrines where built on religious beliefs. However, if such actors encompass comprehensive political doctrines that act against the foundations of liberal democracy, they are seen as intolerant and not party to the overlapping consensus nor to public reason in that respect because they failed the test of reasonableness.

Conclusion

1 Summary

This study presented an assessment of the position of democracy in international law, where it provided that the right to democracy in this context is predominately a procedural one, which encompasses a thin electoral model that cannot provide a full illustration on addressing the issue of political intolerance and the success of democracy especially in transitional societies. The book thus shifted the focus to the presentation of the social contract tradition as the philosophical foundation of modern day democracy in its contemporary sense, where it provided a broad view on the elements and pillars of the concept, beyond the limitations provided in international law.

2 The law: incomplete procedural understanding of democracy

The right to democracy as founded in Articles 21 of the Universal Declaration on Human Rights (UDHR) and 25 of the International Covenant on Civil and Political Rights (ICCPR) as interpreted by the Human Rights Committee is limited to the exercise of periodic free and fair elections. This procedural view cannot defend democracy against its ideologically intolerant enemies, where the lack of substance, defined as a number of mutually reinforcing rights, amounts to a loophole in the system. Therefore, in theory at least, intolerant actors could undoubtedly use elections as a means to reach power and abolish the democratic system.

Wider developments in international law provided a richer understanding of the right to democracy. A substantive view emerged in the aftermath of the collapse of the Soviet Union. The Secretary-General issued a number of substantive reports that reaffirmed the international community's commitment to democracy. Other international and regional bodies and courts delivered a number of compelling declarations and measures to enrich the democracy norm in international law, beyond the procedural sense to include a series of civil and political rights that are mutually reinforcing. However, State practice and the behaviour of international organizations, namely the UN, provide a coherent approach towards the procedural understanding of democracy. This is in the form of the limitation of *democratization measures* to their procedural element, in the form of electoral assistance and technical support. This was indeed the case in the aftermath of the Arab Spring, and contributes nonetheless to the significant conceptual problem associated with the right to democracy in international law.

3 Democratic theory: needs to be extended

The limitations on the right to democracy in international law and the consequent lack of a substantive conceptualization of the term call for a review of the philosophical foundations of democratic government and the citizen and his/her relationship with the State. The theoretical roots of the substantive account of democratic governance are echoed in the contemporary social contract tradition.

The works of John Rawls represent the best contemporary account of the social contract tradition through the introduction of an instrumental right to democracy. This was through the understanding that democratic participation was an instrument and a means to achieve liberty, which is an important principle of justice. His *magnum opus*, *A Theory of Justice*, was the basis of his philosophical interpretation of the theory. To Rawls, a polity aims to achieve two principles of justice, liberty and opportunities, income and wealth. The most important principle for the purpose of this thesis is liberty, which is the subject of the instrumental understanding of democracy. HLA Hart criticized it for being 'too vague'; however, a vague interpretation of the term widens its scope. In other words, Rawls presented the best interpretation of liberty, wherein it is 'only restricted for the sake of another liberty'. In order to achieve liberty in a 'well-ordered democratic society' decisions are made behind a veil of ignorance.

The veil of ignorance doctrine is central to his argument. According to this doctrine, decisions are made for the benefit of the least advantaged individual regardless of his affiliations. Accordingly, citizens, who are the first decision-makers, or their representatives, will not be biased in favour of their religious, linguistic or ethnic communities. Therefore, the veil of ignorance should be seen not only as a prerequisite for democracy, but also, for its final outcome, justice, through the application of its principles, including liberty – widely defined.

In *Political Liberalism*, Rawls presented a very detailed illustration of the pillars of the 'well-ordered democratic society'. The first one is the reasonable citizen. Citizens are reasonable when they see one another as equals in a system of cooperation over generations, and they are able to do so not 'under the pressure of an inferior political or social position' defined as an alternative affiliation to one's community. The importance of this understanding of the citizen is that – as mentioned earlier – he is the first decision-maker in a democratic society.

The second important pillar of a democratic society is the overlapping consensus. It comes from the assumption that there is no comprehensive moral, religious or philosophical doctrine affirmed by all citizens in a democratic society other than the two principles of justice. Hence, an overlapping consensus is when conflicting political groups, with opposing interests and ideologies, agree to and support liberal democratic principles, under a democratic constitutional regime in order to achieve justice.

The third pillar relevant to this analysis is public reason. According to Rawls, the notion is a product of reasonable pluralism, where members of a democratic society debate openly the application of the two principles of justice. The notion does not, therefore, encompass the debate on the enforcement of one's distinctive comprehension of the good, nor is it a platform for the discussion of one's moral or philosophical truths. It comes from the view that liberal democracy is a comprehensive doctrine in its own right, and it cannot encompass other conflicting comprehensive doctrines. Therefore, the whole concept views democracy as an instrument to achieve liberty. The instrumental right makes democracy an end to achieve a moral objective, rather than a means to reach political power as provided in the procedural understanding of the notion.

The contemporary account of the social contract as found in the works of John Rawls was also addressed to a Western audience. Rawls, however, presented some cultural relativism, when he addressed an imagined Muslim nation, Kazanistan, in *The Law of Peoples*. However, that was problematic since in order to achieve cultural relativism Rawls departed from some of his main principles where he tolerated some undemocratic measures. The departure from liberty also encompassed a denial of the instrumental right to democracy he advanced in his original hypothesis.

Therefore, in order to celebrate the end of history, in terms of the right to democracy in international law, the contemporary principles of democracy as echoed in the philosophy of John Rawls need to be incorporated in binding international benchmarks. This needs to be done without any compromise on the principle of liberty, which is the backbone of democracy, and is necessary not only for the maintenance of public international law, but also for the political evolution of mankind at the international level.

Bibliography

Allot P, 'Language, Method and the Nature of International Law' (1971) 45 *British Yearbook of International Law* 103.

Alston P, 'The Historical Origins of the Concept of "General Comments" in Human Rights Law' in LB de Chazournes and VG Debbas (eds), *The International Legal System in Quest of Equity and Universality: Liber Amicorum, Georges Abi-Saab* (Kluwer Law International 2001), 257–75.

Barry B, 'John Rawls and the Priority of Liberty' (1973) 2 *Philosophy & Public Affairs* 274.

Bartelson J, 'The Concept of Sovereignty Revisited' (2006) 17 *EJIL* 463.

Bederman DJ, *Globalization and International Law* (Palgrave MacMillan 2008).

Beitz CR, 'Rawls's Law of Peoples' (2000) 110 *Ethics* 669.

Bell C, 'Power Sharing and Human Rights Law' (2013) 17 *The International Journal of Human Rights* 204.

Berelson B, 'Democratic Theory and Public Opinion' (1952) 16 *Public Opinion Quarterly* 313.

Bodansky D, 'Customary (and not so Customary) International Environmental Law' (1995) 3 *Symposium: International Environmental Laws and Agencies: The Next Generation* 105.

Boerefijin I, 'Towards a Strong System of Supervision: The Human Rights Committee's Role in Reforming the Reports Procedure under Article 40 of the Covenant on Civil and Political Rights' (1995) 17 *HRQ* 766.

Boyle K, 'Human Rights, Religion and Democracy: The Refah Partisi Case' (2004) 1 *Essex Human Rights Review* 1.

Brighouse H, 'Civic Education and Liberal Legitimacy' (1998) 108 *Ethics* 719.

Brownlie I, *Principles of Public International Law* (4th edn, Oxford University Press 1990).

Buchanan A, 'Rawls's Law of Peoples: Rules for a Vanished Westphalian World' (2000) 110 *Ethics* 697.

Buchannan JM, 'The Justice of Natural Liberty' (1978) 5 *Journal of Legal Studies* 1.

Burchill R, 'The Developing International Law of Democracy' (2001) 64 *The Modern Law Review* 123.

——— 'Regional Integration and the Promotion and Protection of Democracy in Asia: Lessons from ASEAN' (2009) 13 *Asian Yearbook of International Law* 113.

Buzan B, R Little and C Jones, *The Logic of Anarchy* (Columbia University Press 1993).

Byers M and S Chesterman, '"You the People": Pro-Democratic Intervention in International Law' in GH Fox and BR Roth (eds), *Democratic Governance in International Law* (Cambridge University Press 2000).

Callejon C, 'Developments at the Human Rights Council in 2007: A Reflection of Its Ambivalence' (2008) 8 *Human Rights Law Review* 323, 331–4.

Cassel D, 'Does International Human Rights Law Make a Difference?' (2001) 2 *Chicago Journal of International Law* 121.

Chodosh HE, 'Neither Treaty Nor Custom: The Emergence of Declarative International Law' (1991) 26 *Texas International Law Journal* 87.

Christiano T, 'An Instrumental Argument for a Human Right to Democracy' (2011) 39 *Philosophy & Public Affairs* 142.

Conte A and R Burchill (eds), *Defining Civil and Political Rights: The Jurisprudence of the United Nations Human Rights Committee* (2nd edn, Ashgate 2009) 97.

Copsey N, 'Changing Course or Changing Clothes? Reflections on the Ideological Evolution of the British National Party 1999–2006' (2007) 41 *Patterns of Prejudice* 61.

Crawford J, 'The Rights of Peoples: "Peoples" or "Governments"?' (1985) 9 *Bulletin of the Australian Society of Legal Philosophy* 136.

Crook M and T Crook, 'The Advent of the Secret Ballot in Britain and France, 1789–1914: From Public Assembly to Private Compartment' (2007) 92 *History* 449.

Dahl RA, *Who Governs?* (Yale University Press 1961).

Dahl RA and CE Lindblom, *Politics, Economics and Welfare* (Harper & Bros 1953).

D'Amato AA, *The Concept of Custom in International Law* (Cornell University Press 1971).

d'Aspremont J, 'Legitimacy of Governments in the Age of Democracy' (2006) 38 *New York University Journal of International Law and Politics* 877.

——— 'Responsibility for Coups in International Law' (2010) 18 *Tulane Journal of International and Comparative Law* 451.

——— 'The Rise and Fall of Democracy Governance in International Law: A Reply to Susan Marks' (2011) 22 *EJIL* 549.

Dauenhauer DP, 'A Good Word for a Modus Vivendi' in V Davion and C Wolf (eds), *The Idea of Political Pluralism: Essays on Rawls* (Rowman & Littlefield 2000).

De Marneffe P, 'Liberalism, Liberty and Neutrality' (1990) 19 *Philosophy & Public Affairs* 253.

Downs A, *An Economic Theory of Democracy* (Harper & Row 1957).

Evans JAJ, 'The Dynamics of Social Change in Radical Right-wing Populist Party Support' (2005) 3 *Comparative European Politics* 76.

Fox GH, 'Democracy, Right to, International Protection' in R Wolfrum (ed.), *Max Planck Encyclopedia of Public International Law* (Oxford University Press 2013).

Fox GH and G Nolte, 'Intolerant Democracies' (1995) 36 *Harvard International Law Journal* 1.
Fox GH and B Roth (eds), *Democratic Governance and International Law* (Cambridge University Press 2000).
——— 'Democracy and International Law' (2001) 27 *Review of International Studies* 327.
Franck TM, 'The Emerging Right to Democratic Governance' (1992) 86 *AJIL* 46.
Freeman M, 'The Problem of Secularism in Human Rights Theory' (2004) 26 *HRQ* 375.
Friedmann W, 'North Sea Continental Cases – A Critique' (1970) 64 *AJIL* 229.
Frohlich N, JA Oppenheimer and CL Eavey, 'Choices of Principles of Distributive Justice in Experimental Groups' (1987) 31 *American Journal of Political Science* 606.
Fukuyama F, *The End of History and the Last Man* (Penguin 1993).
Galston WA, 'Civic Education and Political Participation' (2004) 37 *Political Science and Politics* 263.
Ghandi P, *The Human Rights Committee and the Right of Individual Communication: Law and Practice* (Ashgate 1998).
Goldsmith J, 'Should International Human Rights Law Trump US Domestic Law?' (2000) 1 *Chicago Journal of International Law* 327.
Goodwin-Gill G, *Free and Fair Elections: International Law and Practice* (Inter-Parliamentary Union 1994).
Gorjao P, 'The Legacy and Lessons of the United Nations Transitional Administration in East Timor' (2002) 24 *Contemporary Southeast Asia* 313.
Gross L, 'The Peace of Westphalia' (1948) 42 *AJIL* 20.
Hannum H, 'The Status of the Universal Declaration of Human Rights in National and International Law' (1995/6) 25 *Georgia Journal of International and Comparative Law* 287.
Harsanyi JC, 'Cardinal Utility in Welfare Economics and in the Theory of Risk-taking' (1953) 61 *Journal of Political Economy* 434.
Hart HLA, 'Rawls on Liberty and Its Priority' (1973) 40 *The University of Chicago Law Review* 534.
Hathaway OA, 'Do Human Rights Treaties Make a Difference?' (2002) 111 *Yale Law Journal* 1935.
Held D, 'Law of States, Law of Peoples: Three Models of Sovereignty' (2002) 8 *Legal Theory* 1.
Henkin J, 'Rights: Here and There' (1981) 81 *Columbia Law Review* 1592.
Henkin L (ed.), *The International Bill of Rights: The Covenant on Civil and Political Rights* (Colombia University Press 1981).
Hill L, 'Public Acceptance of Compulsory Voting: Explaining the Australian Case' (2010) 46 *Representation* 425.
Holsti KJ, *International Politics: A Framework of Analysis* (5th edn, Englewood Cliffs 1988).
Hudson C, 'Fisheries and Economic Zones as Customary International Law' (1980) 70 *San Diego Law Review* 661.

Hughes CA, 'Compulsory Voting' (1966) 1 *Australian Journal of Political Science* 83.

Humphrey JP, 'The International Bill of Rights: Scope and Implementation' (1976) 17 *William and Mary Law Review* 527.

——— *No Distant Millennium: The International Law of Human Rights* (UNESCO 1989).

Jones C, 'Global Liberalism: Political of Comprehensive' (2004) 54 *University of Toronto Law Journal* 227.

Joseph S, 'New Procedures Concerning the Human Rights Committee's Examination of State Reports' (1995) 13 *Netherlands Quarterly of Human Rights* 5.

Joseph S, J Schultz and M Castan, *The International Covenant on Civil and Political Rights: Cases, Material, and Commentary* (Oxford University Press 2000).

Kant I, 'An Answer to the Question: What Is Enlightenment?' in HS Reiss (ed.), *Kant: Political Writings* (Cambridge University Press 1970).

Kelsen H, *Principles of International Law* (The Lawbook Exchange 1952).

Kirgis FL Jr., 'Custom in a Sliding Scale' (1987) 81 *AJIL* 146.

Kornhauser W, *The Politics of Mass Society* (Free Press 1959).

Koskenniemi M, 'Intolerant Democracies: A Reaction' (1996) 37 *Harvard International Law Journal* 231.

Kunz JH, 'The Nature of Customary International Law' (1953) 47 *AJIL* 662.

Langlaude S, 'Indoctrination, Secularism, Religious Liberty and the ECHR' (2006) 55 *ICLQ* 929.

Lardy H, 'Citizenship and the Right to Vote' (1997) 17 *Oxford Journal of Legal Studies* 91.

Lauterpacht H, 'The Universal Declaration of Human Rights' (1948) 25 *British Yearbook of International Law* 354.

——— *International Law and Human Rights* (Stevens 1950).

——— *The Development of International Law by the International Court* (Stevens 1958).

Lombardo CE, 'The Making of an Agenda for Democratization: A Speechwriter's View' (2001) 2 *Chicago Journal of International Law* 253.

MacGibbon IC, 'Customary International Law and Acquiescence' (1957) 33 *British Yearbook of International Law* 115.

Mackie G, 'Schumpeter's Leadership Democracy' (2009) 37 *Political Theory* 128.

Macpherson CB, *The Real World of Democracy* (Clarendon Press 1966).

——— *Democratic Theory* (Clarendon Press 1973).

Marks SP, 'From the "Single Confused Page" to the "Decalogue for Six Billion Persons": The Roots of the Universal Declaration of Human Rights in the French Revolution' (1998) 20 *HRQ* 459.

Martin I and A Mayer-Rieckh, 'The United Nations and East Timor: From Self-Determination to State-Building' (2005) 12 *International Peacekeeping* 125.

McAllister I, 'Compulsory Voting, Turnout and Party Advantage in Australia' (1986) 21 *Australian Journal of Political Science* 89.

McGoldrick D, *The Human Rights Committee: Its Role in the Development of the International Covenant on Civil and Political Rights* (Clarendon Press 1994).

Meagher S, 'When Personal Computers Are Transformed into Ballot Boxes: How Internet Elections in Estonia Comply with the United Nations International Covenant on Civil and Political Rights' (2007) 23 *American University International Law Review* 365.

Meron T, *Human Rights Law-Making in the United Nations: A Critique of Instruments and Process* (Clarendon Press 1986).

Merrills JG, *The Development of International Law by the European Court of Human Rights* (Manchester University Press 1993).

Mizok A, 'The Legality of the Fifty-Two Year State of Emergency in Israel' (2001) 7 *University of California Davis Journal of International Law and Policy* 223.

Moellendorf D, 'Constructing the Law of Peoples' (1996) 77 *Pacific Philosophical Quarterly* 132.

Mouffe C, 'The Limits of John Rawls's Pluralism' (2005) 4 *Politics, Philosophy & Economics* 221.

Murphy S, 'Democratic Legitimacy and the Recognition of States and Governments' (1999) 48 *ICLQ* 545.

——— 'Democratic Legitimacy and the Recognition of States and Governments' in GH Fox and BR Roth (eds), *Democratic Governance in International Law* (Cambridge University Press 2000).

Nagel T, 'Rawls and Liberalism' in SR Freeman (ed.), *The Cambridge Companion to Rawls* (Cambridge University Press 2003).

Nowak M, *UN Covenant on Civil and Political Rights: CCPR Commentary* (2nd revised edn, NP Engel 2005).

Ovey C and RCA White, *The European Convention on Human Rights* (4th edn, Oxford University Press 2006).

Parent WA, 'Some Recent Work on the Concept of Liberty' (1974) 11 *American Philosophical Quarterly* 166.

Pechota V, 'The Development of the Covenant on Civil and Political Rights' in L Henkin (ed.), *The International Bill of Rights: The Covenant on Civil and Political Rights* (Colombia University Press 1981).

Porter K, *A History of Suffrage in the United States* (Chicago University Press 1918).

Prior M, 'News vs. Entertainment: How Increasing Media Choice Widens Gaps in Political Knowledge and Turnout' (2005) 49 *American Journal of Political Science* 577.

Rawls J, 'The Law of Peoples' (1993) 20 *Critical Inquiry* 36.

——— *Political Liberalism* (expanded edn, Columbia University Press 1996).

——— 'The Idea of Public Reason Revisited' (1997) 64 *The University of Chicago Law Review* 765.

——— *A Theory of Justice* (revised edn, Harvard University Press 1999).

——— *The Law of Peoples: With the Idea of Public Reason Revisited* (Harvard University Press 2001).

Rehman J, *International Human Rights Law* (2nd edn, Longman 2010) 80.

Ricci DM, 'Democracy Attenuated: Schumpeter, the Process Theory and American Democratic Thought' (1970) 32 *The Journal of Politics* 239.

Rich R, 'Recognition of States: The Collapse of Yugoslavia and the Soviet Union' (1993) 4 *EJIL* 36.

Richardson JE, '"Our England": Discourses of "Race" and Class in Party Election Leaflets' (2008) 18 *Social Semiotics* 321.

Roberts AE, 'Traditional and Modern Approaches to Customary International Law: A Reconciliation' (2001) 95 *AJIL* 757.

Rosberg GM, 'Aliens and Equal Protection: Why Not the Right to Vote?' (1976) 75 *Michigan Law Review* 1093.

Roth BR, 'Democratic Intolerance: Observations on Fox and Nolte' (1996) 37 *Harvard International Law Journal* 235.

——— 'Evaluating Democratic Progress' in GH Fox and BR Roth (eds), *Democratic Governance and International Law* (Cambridge University Press 2000).

——— *Governmental Illegitimacy in International Law* (Oxford University Press 2000).

Ruffert M, 'The Administration of Kosovo and East-Timor by the International Community' (2001) 50 *ICLQ* 613.

Schabas WA, *The Universal Declaration of Human Rights: The Travaux Préparatoires* (Cambridge University Press 2013).

Schachter O, *International Law in Theory and Practice* (Martinus Nijhoff 1991).

Schubert G, *The Public Interest* (Free Press 1962).

Schumpeter JA, *Capitalism, Socialism and Democracy* (Harper & Row 1942).

Smith S, 'Reasons of State' in D Held and C Pollitt (eds), *New Forms of Democracy* (Sage 1987).

Smith TM, 'Between Allah and Atatürk: Liberal Islam in Turkey' (2005) 9 *The International Journal of Human Rights* 307.

Sohn LB, 'The Human Rights Law of the Charter' (1977) 12 *Texas International Law Journal* 129.

Stahn C, 'Constitution without a State? Kosovo under the United Nations Constitutional Framework for Self-Government' (2001) 14 *Leiden Journal of International Law* 531.

Steiner HJ, 'Political Participation as a Human Right' (1988) 1 *Harvard Human Rights Yearbook* 77.

Steiner HJ, P Alston and R Goodman, *International Human Rights in Context: Law, Politics, Morals* (3rd edn, Oxford University Press 2008).

Still JW, 'Political Equality and Electoral Systems' (1984) 91 *Ethics* 375.

Strohmeyer H, 'Collapse and Reconstruction of a Judicial System: The United Nations Missions in Kosovo and East Timor' (2001) 95 *AJIL* 46.

Tamanaha BZ, 'Understanding Legal Pluralism: Past to Present, Local to Global' (2007) 29 *Sydney Law Review* 19.

Tan KC, 'Liberal Toleration in Rawls's Law of Peoples' (1998) 108 *Ethics* 276.

——— *Toleration, Diversity, and Global Justice* (Pennsylvania State University Press 2000).

Tardu ME, 'United Nations Response to Gross Violations of Human Rights: The 1503 Procedure' (1980) 20 *Santa Carla Law Review* 559.

Tesón FR, 'The Rawlsian Theory of International Law' (1995) 9 *Ethics & International Affairs* 79.

——— *A Philosophy of International Law* (Westview 1998).

Thornberry P, *International Law and the Rights of Minorities* (Clarendon Press 1991).

Truman D, *The Governmental Process* (Knopf 1951).

Tulkens F, 'The European Convention on Human Rights and Church-State Relations: Pluralism vs. Pluralism' (2008) 30 *Cardozo Law Review* 2575.

Vermeule A, 'Veil of Ignorance Rules in Constitutional Law' (2001) 111 *The Yale Law Journal* 405.

Vidmar J, *Democratic Statehood in International Law: The Emergence of New States in Post-Cold War Practice* (Hart 2013).

Walker JL, 'A Critique of the Elitist Theory of Democracy' (1966) 60 *The American Political Science Review* 285.

Wheatley S, 'Democracy in International Law: A European Perspective' (2002) 51 *ICLQ* 225.

——— 'Deliberative Democracy and Minorities' (2003) 14 *EJIL* 507.

——— *Democracy, Minorities and International Law* (Cambridge University Press 2005).

White ND, 'The United Nations and Democracy Assistance: Developing Practice within a Constitutional Framework' in P Burnell (ed.), *Democracy Assistance: International Co-operation for Democratization* (Psychology Press 2002) 67–89.

Wolin SS, 'The Liberal/Democratic Divide on Rawls's *Political Liberalism*' (1996) 24 *Political Theory* 97.

Zaring D, 'International Law by Other Means: The Twilight Existence of International Financial Regulatory Organizations' (1998) 33 *Texas International Law Journal* 281.

Index

acceptance as law 16
Article 25, ICCPR 36–47; electronic elections 41–2; equal access to public services 42; multi-party system 45; option not to vote 41; political parties 43–4; procedural right to democracy 47; right of citizens 38–9; right to democracy 37; right to free and fair elections 36; right to political participation 36–47; right to stand for election 43–7; right to vote 39–42; secret ballot 41; universal suffrage 39–40
Article 21, UDHR: binding status 22; democracy, and 27; drafting history 23–5; 'every citizen' 23–4; first generation of human rights 23; political participation 25; substance 22–5; *travaux preparatoires* 22–5

Buchanan, Allan 87–8

citizen: significance of idea 90
civic education 54
Commonwealth 59–60
constitutional consensus 76–7
constitutions 76–7
Continental Shelf Cases 16
Crawford, James: peoples, on 83
cultural relativism 96

decent society 86
declarations: international custom, and 21
democracy: Article 21 UDHR, and 27; definition 57; full understanding of notion of 50; nature of 56; set of rights to be enforced collectively 58
democracy and the citizen 66–92
democratic entitlement 9–10
democratic theory: extension, need for 94–6; *Refah* principle, and 7–9
DFFE 52–4

ECOSOC 22; monitoring mechanism 25–6
election management 55
electoral dispute settlement 55
electronic elections 41–2
equal access to public services 42
escape from liberty 81–9
European Court of Human Rights 59–63; pluralism, and 60–1; political parties, and 61–3; substantive right to democracy, and 52

first generation of human rights 23
Fox, Gregory 5, 50–1
Franck, Thomas 2
free and fair elections, right to 36
French Declaration of the Rights of Man and of Citizen 24

Human Rights Committee 2–3, 4, 33–6; composition 33; general comments 34; increased role, need for 36; mechanisms of implementation 33; outreach 35; political considerations 35; role of UN Secretary-General, and 33

incomplete procedural understanding of democracy 93–4

International Court of Justice: Article 38 15
International Covenant on Civil and Political Rights (ICCPR) 1–2, 29–48; Article 25 4–5, 36–47 *see also* Article 25, ICCPR; background 31–3; context 31–3; derogations 31–3; importance of 30; mechanisms of implementation 33; scope 29–30; state-reporting mechanisms 34–5
international custom: declarations, and 21
international customary law 13–28; modern understanding of 20–1; right to democracy in 13–28
international organizations 55–9; role in redefinition of right to democracy 55–9

Kant, Immanuel: *What is Enlightenment* 78

liberalism: meaning 70
liberty: nature of 90–1; vagueness of 70; value of 70
liberty behind a veil of ignorance 67–72

Maastricht Treaty 59
media access 54
multi–party system 45

NGOs: role of 35–6
Nolte, Georg 50–1
non–liberal peoples 85–6

OAS 59
overlapping consensus 75–8; exclusions 76; rival political groups, and 77

participation in democratic process 91
political participation: UDHR, and 25
political parties 43–4
procedural right to democracy 13–15
procedural shortcomings 52–5
procedures of democracy 6
public reason 78–81, 95; objective of 79; religion, and 80; secular reason and values, and 80; subject of 79

Rawls, John 10, 66–92; *A Theory of Justice* 67–72; criteria of rationalism 69; framework for instrumental right to democracy 66–7; kinds of internal governments, on 82; liberty, on 68–9; overlapping consensus 75–8; peoples, on 82; *Political Liberalism* 73; sovereignty, on 83–4; system of international cooperation, on 89; *The Idea of Public Reason Revisited* 79–80; *The Law of Peoples* 81–9; toleration approach 88
realistic Utopia 85
reasonable citizen 73–5; veil of ignorance, and 74; well–ordered democratic society, and 75
reasonable pluralism 78–9
reasonableness: nature of 74
Refah principle 7–9; democratic theory, and 7–9
regional organizations 59–63
religion: public reason, and 80
right to democracy in international conventions 29–48
right to vote 39–42
rival political groups: overlapping consensus, and 77

Schumpeter, Joseph 13–14
secret ballot 41
secularism 91–2
social contract: assessment in contemporary sense 90
social contract theory 68
sovereignty 83–4
state practice 16–17; proof of 20
substantive right to democracy 49–65; Cold War, and 50; definition 49; European Court of Human Rights, and 52; procedural shortcomings 52–5

Tan, Kok–Char 87
Teson, Fernando 87
toleration of non–liberal peoples 85

UN Charter 19
UN Commission on Human Rights: *Promotion of the Right to Democracy* 57–8
United Nations Millennium Declaration 59
Universal Declaration of Human Rights UDHR) 1, 10, 17–25;

Article 21 3–4 *see also* Article 21, UDHR; *jus cogens* character 21–2; lack of effective enforcement mechanism 26; legal value of 18–22; monitoring mechanism 25–6; range of rights 18; significance of 17–18; traditional international customary law, and 20; UN Charter, and 19
universal suffrage 39–40
UN Secretary-General: *Agenda for Democratization* 56

veil of ignorance doctrine 66–7, 68, 71–2, 84–5, 95; flexible, need for 89; reasonable citizen, and 73–5
Vienna Declaration and Programme of Action 6, 57

Well-ordered democratic society 75, 95

For Product Safety Concerns and Information please contact our EU
representative GPSR@taylorandfrancis.com
Taylor & Francis Verlag GmbH, Kaufingerstraße 24, 80331 München, Germany

www.ingramcontent.com/pod-product-compliance
Ingram Content Group UK Ltd.
Pitfield, Milton Keynes, MK11 3LW, UK
UKHW021957180926
475701UK00003B/65
* 9 7 8 0 3 6 7 1 9 3 4 7 8 *